THE CYNIC'S WORD BOOK

THE CYNIC'S WORD BOOK

BY

AMBROSE BIERCE

ISBN 978-1-4357-4932-0

PREFACE

WITH reference to certain actual and possible questions of priority and originality, it may be explained that this Word Book was begun in the San Francisco "Wasp" in the year 1881, and has been continued, in a desultory way, in several journals and periodicals. As it was no part of the author's purpose to define all the words in the language, or even to make a complete alphabetical series, the stopping-place of the book was determined by considerations of bulk. In the event of this volume proving acceptable to that part of the reading public to which in humility it is addressed — enlightened souls who prefer dry wines to sweet, sense to sentiment, good English to slang, and wit to humor — there may possibly be another if the author be spared for the compiling.

A conspicuous, and it is hoped not unpleasing, feature of the book is its abundant illustrative quotations from eminent poets, chief of whom is that learned and ingenious cleric, Father Gassalasca Jape, S. J., whose lines bear his initials. To Father Jape's kindly encouragement and assistance the author of the prose text is greatly indebted.

A. B.

Washington, D. C.,
May, 1906

THE CYNIC'S WORD BOOK

The Cynic's Word Book

A

ABASEMENT, *n.* A decent and customary mental attitude in the presence of wealth or power. Peculiarly appropriate in an employé when addressing an employer.

ABATIS, *n.* Rubbish in front of a fort, to prevent the rubbish outside from molesting the rubbish inside.

ABDICATION, *n.* An act whereby a sovereign attests his sense of the high temperature of the throne.

Poor Isabella 's dead, whose abdication
Set all tongues wagging in the Spanish nation.
For that performance 't were unfair to scold her:
She wisely left a throne too hot to hold her.
To History she 'll be no royal riddle —
Merely a plain parched pea that jumped the griddle.

G. J.

ABDOMEN, *n.* The temple of the god Stomach, in whose worship, with sacrificial rights, all true men engage. From women this ancient faith commands but a stammering assent. They sometimes minister at the altar in a half-hearted and inefficient way, but true reverence for the one deity that men really adore they know not. If woman had a free hand in the world's marketing the race would become graminivorous.

ABILITY, *n.* The natural equipment to accomplish some small part of the meaner ambitions distinguishing able men from dead ones. In the last analysis ability is commonly found to consist mainly in a high degree of solemnity. Perhaps, however, this impressive quality is rightly appraised; it is no easy task to be solemn.

ABNORMAL, *adj.* Not conforming to standard. In matters of thought and conduct, to be independent is to be abnormal, to be abnormal is to be detested. Wherefore the lexicographer adviseth a striving toward a straiter resemblance to the Average Man than he hath to himself. Who so attaineth thereto shall have peace, the prospect of death and the hope of Hades.

ABORIGINES, *n.* Persons of little worth found cumbering the soil of a newly discovered country. They soon cease to cumber; they fertilize.

ABRACADABRA.

By *Abracadabra* we signify
  An infinite number of things.
'T is the answer to What? and How? and Why?
And Whence? and Whither? — a word whereby
  The Truth (with the comfort it brings)
Is open to all who grope in night,
Crying for Wisdom's holy light.

Whether the word is a verb or a noun
  Is knowledge beyond my reach.
I only know that 't is handed down
    From sage to sage,
    From age to age —
  An immortal part of speech!

Of an ancient man the tale is told
That he lived to be ten centuries old,
In a cave on a mountain side.
(True, he finally died.)
The fame of his wisdom filled the land,
For his head was bald and you 'll understand
His beard was long and white
And his eyes uncommonly bright.

Philosophers gathered from far and near
To sit at his feet and hear and hear,
Though he never was heard
To utter a word
But "*Abracadabra, abracadab,*
Abracada, abracad.
Abraca, abrac, abra, ab!"
'T was all he had,
'T was all they wanted to hear, for each
Made copious notes of the mystical speech
Which they published next —
A trickle of text
In a meadow of commentary.
Mighty big books were these,
In number, as leaves of trees;
In learning, remarkable — very!

He 's dead,
As I said,
And the books of the sages have perished,
But his wisdom is sacredly cherished.

In "*Abracadabra*" it solemnly rings,
Like an ancient bell that forever swings.
Oh, I love to hear
That word make clear
Humanity's General Sense of Things.
Jamrach Holobom.

ABRIDGE, *v. t.* To shorten.

"When in the course of human events it becomes necessary for a people to abridge their king, a decent respect for the opinions of mankind requires that they should declare the causes which impel them to the separation." — *Oliver Cromwell.*

ABRUPT, *adj.* Sudden, without ceremony, like the arrival of a cannon-shot and the departure of the soldier whose interests are most affected by it. Dr. Samuel Johnson beautifully said of another author's ideas that they were "concatenated without abruption."

ABSCOND, *v. i.* To "move" in a mysterious way, commonly with the property of another.

Spring beckons! All things to the call respond;
The trees are leaving and cashiers abscond.

Phela Orm.

ABSENT, *adj.* Peculiarly exposed to the tooth of detraction; vilified; hopelessly in the wrong; superseded in the consideration and affection of another.

To men a man is but a mind. Who cares
What face he carries or what form he wears?
But woman's body is the woman. Oh,
Stay thou, my sweetheart, and do never go.
But heed the warning words the sage hath said:
A woman absent is a woman dead.

Jogo Tyree.

ABSENTEE, *n.* A person with an income who has had the forethought to remove himself from the sphere of exaction.

ABSOLUTE, *adj.* Independent, irresponsible. An absolute monarchy is one in which the sovereign does as he pleases so long as he pleases the assassins. Not many absolute monarchies are left, most of them having been replaced by limited monarchies, where the sovereigns' power for evil (and for good) is greatly curtailed, and by republics, which are governed by chance.

ABSTAINER, *n.* A weak person who yields to the temptation of denying himself a pleasure. A Total Abstainer is one who abstains from everything, but abstention, and especially from inactivity in the affairs of others.

Said a man to a crapulent youth: "I thought
You a total abstainer, my son."
"So I am, so I am," said the scapegrace caught —
"But not, sir, a bigoted one."

G. J.

ABSURDITY, *n.* A statement or belief manifestly inconsistent with one's own opinion.

ACADEME, *n.* An ancient school where morality and philosophy were taught.

ACADEMY, *n.* [from Academe]. A modern school where football is taught.

ACCIDENT, *n.* An inevitable occurrence due to the action of immutable natural laws.

ACCOMPLICE, *n.* One associated with another in a crime, having guilty knowledge and complicity, as an attorney who defends a criminal, knowing him guilty. This view of the attorney's position in the matter has not hitherto commanded the assent of attorneys, no one having offered them a fee for assenting.

ACCORD, *n.* Harmony.

ACCORDION, *n.* An instrument in harmony with the sentiments of an assassin.

ACCOUNTABILITY, *n.* The mother of caution.

"My accountability, bear in mind,"
Said the Grand Vizier: "Yes, yes."
Said the Shah: "I do—'t is the only kind
Of ability you possess."

Joram Tate.

ACCUSE, *v. t.* To affirm another's guilt or unworth; most commonly as a justification of ourselves for having wronged him.

ACEPHALOUS, *adj.* In the surprising condition of the Crusader who absently pulled at his forelock some hours after a Saracen scimitar had, unconsciously to him, passed through his neck, as related by the Prince de Joinville.

ACHIEVEMENT, *n.* The death of endeavor and the birth of disgust.

ACKNOWLEDGE, *v. t.* To confess. To acknowledge one another's faults is the highest duty imposed by our love of truth.

ACQUAINTANCE, *n.* A person whom we know well enough to borrow from, but not well enough to lend to. A degree of friendship called slight when its object is poor or obscure, and "intimate" when he is rich or famous.

ACTUALLY, *adv.* Perhaps; possibly.

ADAGE, *n.* Boned wisdom for weak teeth.

ADAMANT, *n.* A mineral frequently found beneath a corset. Soluble in solicitate of gold.

ADDER, *n.* A species of snake. So called from its habit of adding funeral outlays to the other expenses of living.

ADHERENT, *n.* A follower who has not yet obtained all that he expects to get.

ADMINISTRATION, *n.* An ingenious abstraction in politics, designed to receive the kicks and cuffs due to the premier or president. A man of straw, proof against bad-egging and dead-catting.

ADMIRABILITY, *n.* My kind of ability, as distinguished from your kind of ability.

ADMIRAL, *n.* That part of a war-ship which does the talking while the figure-head does the thinking.

ADMIRATION, *n.* Our polite recognition of another's resemblance to ourselves.

ADMONITION, *n.* Gentle reproof, as with a meat-axe. Friendly warning.

> Consigned, by way of admonition,
> His soul forever to perdition.
>
> *Judibras.*

ADORE, *v. t.* To venerate expectantly.

ADVICE, *n.* The smallest current coin.

"The man was in such deep distress,"
Said Tom, "that I could do no less
Than give him good advice." Said Jim:
"If less could have been done for him
I know you well enough, my son,
To know that 's what you would have done."

Jebel Jocordy.

AFFIANCED, *pp.* Fitted with an ankle-ring for the ball-and-chain.

AFFLICTION, *n.* An acclimatizing process preparing the soul for another and bitter world.

AFRICAN, *n.* A nigger that votes our way.

AGE, *n.* That period of life in which we compound for the vices that remain by reviling those that we have no longer the vigor to commit.

AGITATOR, *n.* A statesman who shakes the fruit trees of his neighbors — to dislodge the worms.

AIM, *n.* The task we set our wishes to.

"Cheer up! Have you no aim in life?"
She tenderly inquired.
"An aim? Well, no, I have n't, wife;
The fact is — I have fired."

G. J.

AIR, *n.* That nutritious substance so abundantly supplied by a bountiful Providence for the fattening of the poor.

ALDERMAN, *n.* An ingenious criminal who covers his secret thieving with a pretence of open marauding.

ALIEN, *n.* An American sovereign in his probationary state.

ALLAH, *n.* The Mahometan Supreme Being, as distinguished from the Christian, Jewish, etc.

Allah's good laws I faithfully have kept,
And ever for the sins of man have wept;
And sometimes kneeling in the temple I
Have reverently crossed my hands and slept.

Junker Barlow.

ALLEGIANCE, *n.*

This thing Allegiance, as I suppose,
Is a ring fitted in the subject's nose,
Whereby that organ is kept rightly pointed
To smell the sweetness of the Lord's anointed.

G. J.

ALLIANCE, *n.* In international politics, the union of two thieves who have their hands so deeply inserted in each other's pocket that they cannot separately plunder a third.

ALLIGATOR, *n.* The crocodile of America, superior in every respect to the crocodile of the effete monarchies of the Old World. Herodotus says the Indus is, with one exception, the only river that produces crocodiles, but they appear to have gone West and grown up with the other rivers. From the notches on his back the alligator is called a sawrian.

ALONE, *adj.* In bad company.

In contact, lo! the flint and steel,
By spark and flame, the thought reveal
That he the metal, she the stone,
Had cherished secretly alone.

Booley Fito.

ALTAR, *n.* The place whereon the priest formerly ravelled out the small intestine of the sacrificial victim for purposes of divination and cooked its flesh for the gods. The word is now seldom used, except with reference to the sacrifice of their liberty and peace by a male and a female fool.

They stood before the altar and supplied
The fire themselves in which their fat was fried.
In vain the sacrifice! — no god will claim
An offering burnt with an unholy flame.

M. P. Noppat.

AMBIDEXTROUS, *adj.* Able to pick with equal skill a right-hand pocket or a left.

AMBITION, *n.* An overmastering desire to be villified by enemies while living and made ridiculous by friends when dead.

AMNESTY, *n.* The State's magnanimity to those offenders whom it would be too expensive to punish.

ANOINT, *v. t.* To grease. To consecrate a king or other great functionary already sufficiently slippery.

As sovereigns are anointed by the priesthood,
So pigs to lead the populace are greased good.

Judibras.

ANTIPATHY, *n.* The sentiment inspired by one's friend's friend.

APHORISM, *n.* A brief statement, bald in style and flat in sense.

The flabby wine-skin of a brain
That, spilling once and filled again,
Voids from its impotent abysm
The driblet of an aphorism.

"*The Mad Philosopher*," *1697.*

APOLOGIZE, *v. i.* To lay the foundation for a future offence.

APOSTATE, *n.* A leech who, having penetrated the shell of a turtle only to find the creature has long been dead, deems it expedient to form a new attachment to a fresh turtle.

APOTHECARY, *n.* The physician's accomplice, undertaker's benefactor and grave worm's provider.

When Jove sent blessings to all men that are,
And Mercury conveyed them in a jar,
That friend of tricksters introduced by stealth
Disease for the apothecary's health,
Whose gratitude impelled him to proclaim:
"My deadliest drug shall bear my patron's name!"

G. J.

APPEAL, *v. t.* In law, to put the dice into the box for another throw.

APPETITE, *n.* An instinct thoughtfully implanted by Providence as a solution to the labor question.

APPLAUSE, *n.* The echo of a platitude.

APRIL FOOL, *n.* The March fool with another month added to his folly.

ARBITRATION, *n.* A modern device for promoting strife by substituting for an original dispute a score of inevitable disagreements as to the manner of submitting it for settlement.

ARCHBISHOP, *n.* An ecclesiastical dignitary one point holier than a bishop.

If I were a jolly archbishop,
On Fridays I'd eat all the fish up —
Salmon and flounders and smelts;
On other days everything else.

Jodo Rem.

ARCHITECT, *n.* One who drafts a plan of your house, and plans a draft of your money; who estimates the whole cost, and himself costs the whole estimate.

ARDOR, *n.* The quality that distinguishes love without knowledge.

ARENA, *n.* In politics, an imaginary rat-pit, in which the statesman wrestles with his record.

ARISTOCRACY, *n.* Government by the best men. (In this sense the word is obsolete; so is that kind of government.) Fellows that wear downy hats and clean shirts — guilty of education and suspected of bank accounts.

ARMOR, *n.* The kind of clothing worn by a man whose tailor is a blacksmith.

ARRAYED, *pp.* Drawn up and given an orderly disposition, as a rioter hanged to a lamp-post.

ARREST, *v. t.* Formally to detain one accused of unusualness.

God made the world in six days and was arrested on the seventh. — *The Unauthorized Version.*

ARSENIC, *n.* A kind of cosmetic greatly affected by the ladies, whom it greatly affects in turn.

> "Eat arsenic? Yes, all you get,"
> Consenting, he did speak up;
> "'T is better you should eat it, pet,
> Than put it in my teacup."
>
> *Joel Huck.*

ART, *n.* This word has no definition. Its origin is related as follows by the ingenious Father Gassalasca Jape, S. J.

One day a wag — what would the wretch be at? —
Shifted a letter of the cipher RAT,
And said it was a god's name! Straight arose
Fantastic priests and postulants (with shows,
And mysteries, and mummeries, and hymns,
And disputations dire that lamed their limbs)
To serve his temple and maintain the fires,
Expound the law, manipulate the wires.
Amazed, the populace the rites attend,
Believe whate'er they cannot comprehend,
And, inly edified to learn that two
Half-hairs joined so and so (as Art can do)
Have sweeter values and a grace more fit
Than Nature's hairs that never have been split,
Bring cates and wines forsacrificial feasts,
And sell their garments to support the priests.

ARTLESSNESS, *n.* A certain engaging quality to which women attain by long study and severe practice upon the admiring male, who is pleased to fancy it resembles the candid simplicity of his young.

ASPERSE, *v. t.* Maliciously to ascribe to another vicious actions which one has not had the temptation and opportunity to commit.

ASS, *n.* A public singer with a good voice but no ear. In Virginia City, Nevada, he is called the Washoe Canary, in Dakota, the Senator, and everywhere the Donkey. The animal is widely and variously celebrated in the literature, art, and religion of every age and country; no other so engages and fires the human imagination as this noble vertebrate. Indeed, it is doubted by some (Ramasilus, *lib. II., De Clem.*, and C. Stantatus, *De Temperamente*) if it is not a god; and as such we know it was worshipped by the Etruscans, and, if we may believe Macrobius, by the Capasians also. Of the only two animals admitted into the Mahometan Paradise along with the souls of men, the ass that carried Balaam is one, the dog of the Seven Sleepers the other. This is no small distinction. From what has been written about this beast might be compiled a library of great splendor and magnitude, rivaling that of the Shakspearean cult, and that which clusters about the Bible. It may be said, generally, that all literature is more or less Asinine.

"Hail, holy Ass!" the quiring angels sing;
"Priest of Unreason, and of Discords King!
Great co-Creator, let Thy glory shine:
God made all else, the Mule — the Mule is thine!"

G. J.

AUCTIONEER, *n.* The man who proclaims with a hammer that he has picked a pocket with his tongue.

AUSTRALIA, *n.* A country lying in the South Sea, whose industrial and commercial development has been unspeakably retarded by an unfortunate dispute among geographers as to whether it is a continent or an island.

AVERNUS, *n.* The lake by which the ancients entered the infernal regions. The fact that access to the infernal regions was obtained by a lake is believed by the learned Marcus Ansello Scrutator to have suggested the Christian rite of baptism by immersion. This, however, has been shown by Lactantius to be an error.

Facilis descensus Averni,
The poet remarks; and the sense
Of it is that when down hill I turn I
Will get more of punches than pence.
Jehal Dai Lupe.

AVERSION, *n.* The feeling that one has for the plate after he has eaten its contents, madam.

B

BAAL, *n.* A deity formerly much worshipped under various names. As Baal he was popular with the Phœnicians; as Belus or Bel he had the honor to be served by the priest Berosus, who wrote the famous account of the Deluge; as Babel he had a tower partly erected to his glory on the Plain of Shinar. From Babel comes our English word "babble." Under whatever name worshipped, Baal is the Sun-god. As Beëlzebub he is the god of flies, which are begotten of the sun's rays on stagnant water. In Physicia Baal is still worshipped as Bolus, and as Belly he is adored and served with abundant sacrifice by the priests of Guttle and Swig.

BABE, or BABY, *n.* A misshapen creature of no particular age, sex, or condition, chiefly remarkable for the violence of the sympathies and antipathies it excites in others, itself without sentiment or emotion. There have been famous babes; for example, little Moses, from whose adventure in the bulrushes the Egyptian hierophants of seven centuries before doubtless derived their idle tale of the child Osiris being preserved on a floating lotus leaf.

> Ere babes were invented
> The girls were contented.
> Now man is tormented
> Until to buy babes he has squandered
> His money. And so I have pondered
> This thing, and thought may be
> 'T were better that Baby
> The First had been eagled or condored.
>
> *Ro Amil.*

BACCHUS, *n.* A convenient deity invented by the ancients as an excuse for getting drunk.

> Is public worship, then, a sin,
> That for devotions paid to Bacchus
> The lictors dare to run us in,
> And resolutely thump and whack us?
>
> *Horace.*

BACK, *n.* That part of your friend which it is your privilege to contemplate in your adversity.

BACKBITE, *v. t.* To "speak of a man as you find him" when he can't find you.

BAIT, *n.* A preparation that renders the hook more palatable. The best kind is beauty.

BAPTISM, *n.* A sacred rite of such efficacy that he who finds himself in heaven without having undergone it will be unhappy forever. It is performed with water in two ways — by immersion, or plunging, and by aspersion, or sprinkling.

> But whether the plan of immersion
> Is better than simple aspersion
> Let those immersed
> And those aspersed
> Decide by the Authorized Version,
> And by matching their agues tertian.
>
> *G. J.*

BAROMETER, *n.* An ingenious instrument which indicates what kind of weather we are having.

BARRACK, *n.* A house in which soldiers enjoy a portion of that of which it is their business to deprive others.

BASILISK, *n.* The cockatrice. A sort of serpent hatched from the egg of a cock. The basilisk had a bad eye, and its glance was fatal. Many infidels deny this creature's existence, but Semprello Aurator saw and handled one that had been blinded by lightning as a punishment for having fatally gazed on a lady of rank whom Jupiter loved. Juno afterward restored the reptile's sight and hid it in a cave. Nothing is so well attested by the ancients as the existence of the basilisk, but the cocks have stopped laying eggs.

BASTINADO, *n.* The act of walking on wood without exertion.

BATH, *n.* A kind of mystic ceremony substituted for religious worship, with what spiritual efficacy has not been determined.

> The man who taketh a steam bath
> He loseth all the skin he hath,
> And, for he 's boiled a brilliant red,
> Thinketh to cleanliness he 's wed,
> Forgetting that his lungs he 's soiling
> With dirty vapors of the boiling.
>
> *Richard Gwow.*

BATTLE, *n.* A method of untying with the teeth a political knot that would not yield to the tongue.

BEARD, *n.* The hair that is commonly cut off by those who justly execrate the absurd Chinese custom of shaving the head.

BEAUTY, *n.* The power by which a woman charms a lover and terrifies a husband.

BEFRIEND, *v. t.* To make an ingrate.

BEG, *v.* To ask for something with an earnestness proportioned to the belief that it will not be given.

Who is that, father?
A mendicant, child,
Haggard, morose, and unaffable — wild!
See how he glares through the bars of his cell!
With Citizen Mendicant all is not well.

Why did they put him there, father?
Because
Obeying his belly he struck at the laws.

His belly?
Oh, well, he was starving, my boy —
A state in which, doubtless, there 's little of joy.
No bite had he eaten for days, and his cry
Was "Bread!" ever "Bread!"
What 's the matter with pie?

With little to wear, he had nothing to sell;
To beg was unlawful — improper as well.

Why did n't he work?
He would even have done that,
But men said: "Get out!" and the State remarked: "Scat!"
I mention these incidents merely to show
That the vengeance he took was uncommonly low.
Revenge, at the best, is the act of a Siou,
But for trifles —
Pray what did bad Mendicant do?

Stole two loaves of bread to replenish his lack
And tuck out the belly that clung to his back.

Is that *all* father dear?

There is little to tell:
They sent him to jail, and they 'll send him to—
well,
The company 's better than here we can boast,
And there 's—
Bread for the needy, dear father?
Um—toast.
Atka Mip.

BEGGAR, *n.* One who has relied on the assistance of his friends.

BEHAVIOR, *n.* Conduct, as determined, not by principle, but by breeding. The word seems to be somewhat loosely used in Dr. Jamrach Holobom's translation of the following lines in the *Dies Iræ:*

Recordare, Jesu pie,
Quod sum causa tuæ viæ
Ne me perdas illa die.

Pray remember, sacred Savior,
Whose the thoughtless hand that gave your
Death-blow. Pardon such behavior.

BELLADONNA, *n.* In Italian a beautiful lady; in English a deadly poison.

A striking example of the essential identity of the two tongues.

BENEDICTINES, *n.* An order of monks, otherwise known as black friars.

He thought it a crow, but it turned out to be
A monk of St. Benedict croaking a text.
"Here 's one of an order of cooks," said he —
"Black friars in this world, fried black in the next."

"*The Devil on Earth*" (*London, 1712*).

BENEFACTOR, *n.* One who makes heavy purchases of ingratitude, without, however, materially affecting the price, which is still within the means of all.

BERENICE'S HAIR, *n.* A constellation (*Coma Berenices*) named in honor of one who sacrificed her hair to save her husband.

Her locks an ancient lady gave
Her loving husband's life to save;
And men — they honored so the dame —
Upon some stars bestowed her name.

But to our modern married fair,
Who 'd give their lords to save their hair,
No stellar recognition 's given.
There are not stars enough in heaven.

G. J.

BIGAMY, *n.* A mistake in taste for which the wisdom of the future will adjudge a punishment called trigamy.

BIGOT, *n.* One who is obstinately and zealously attached to an opinion that you do not entertain.

BILLINGSGATE, *n.* The invective of an opponent.

BIRTH, *n.* The first and direst of disasters. As to the nature of it there appears to be no uniformity. Castor and Pollux were born from the egg. Pallas came out of a skull. Galatea was once a block of stone. Peresilis, who wrote in the tenth century, avers that he grew up out of the ground where a priest had spilled holy water. It is known that Arimaxus was derived from a hole in the earth, made by a stroke of lightning. Leucomedon was the son of a cavern in Mount Ætna, and I have myself seen a man come out of a wine cellar.

BLACKGUARD, *n.* A man whose qualities, prepared for the display like a box of berries in a market — the fine ones on top — have been opened on the wrong side. An inverted gentleman.

BLANK-VERSE, *n.* Unrhymed iambic pentameters — the most difficult kind of English verse to write acceptably; a kind, therefore, much affected by those who cannot acceptably write any kind.

BODY-SNATCHER, *n.* A robber of grave-worms. One who supplies the young physicians with that with which the old physicians have supplied the undertaker. The hyena.

"One night," a doctor said, "last fall,
I and my comrades, four in all,
When visiting a grave-yard stood
Within the shadow of a wall.

"While waiting for the moon to sink
We saw a wild hyena slink
About a new-made grave, and then
Begin to excavate its brink!

"Shocked by the horrid act, we made
A sally from our ambuscade,
And, falling on the unholy beast,
Dispatched him with a pick and spade."

Bettel K. Jhones.

BONDSMAN, *n.* A fool who, having property of his own, undertakes to become responsible for that entrusted to another.

Philippe of Orleans wishing to appoint one of his favorites, a dissolute nobleman, to a high office, asked him what security he would be able to give. "I need no bondsmen," he replied, "for I can give you my word of honor." "And pray what may be the value of that?" inquired the amused Regent.

"Monsieur, it is worth its weight in gold."

BORE, *n.* A person who talks when you wish him to listen.

BOTANY, *n.* The science of vegetables—those that are not good to eat, as well as those that are. It deals largely with their flowers, which are commonly badly designed, inartistic in color, and ill-smelling.

BOTTLE-NOSED, *adj.* Having a nose created in the image of its maker.

BOUNDARY, *n.* In political geography, an imaginary line between two nations, separating the imaginary rights of one from the imaginary rights of the other.

BOUNTY, *n.* The liberality of one who has all things, in permitting one who has nothing to get all he can.

"A single swallow, it is said, devours

ten millions of insects every year. The supplying of these insects I take to be a signal instance of the Creator's bounty in providing for the lives of His creatures."

Henry Ward Beecher.

BRAHMA, *n.* He who created the Hindoos, who are preserved by Vishnu and destroyed by Siva — a rather neater division of labor than is found among the deities of some other nations. The Abracadabranese, for example, are created by Sin, maintained by Theft and destroyed by Folly. The priests of Brahma, like those of the Abracadabranese, are holy and learned men who are never naughty.

O Brahma, thou rare old Divinity,
First Person of the Hindoo Trinity,
You sit there so calm and securely,
With feet folded up so demurely —
You 're the First Person Singular, surely.

Polydore Smith.

BRAIN, *n.* An apparatus with which we think that we think. That which distinguishes the man who is content to *be* something from the man who wishes to *do* something. A man of great wealth, or one who has been pitchforked into high station, has commonly such a headful of brain that his neighbors cannot keep their hats on. In our civilization, and under our republican form of government, brain is so highly honored that it is rewarded by exemption from the cares of office.

BRANDY, *n.* A cordial composed of one part thunder-and-lightning, one part remorse, two parts bloody murder, one part death-hell-and-the-grave and four parts clarified Satan. Dose, a headful all the time. Brandy is said, by Carlyle, I think, to be the drink of heroes. Only a hero will venture to drink it.

BRIDE, *n.* A woman with a fine prospect of happiness behind her.

BRUTE, *n.* See HUSBAND.

C

CAABA, *n.* A large stone presented by the archangel Gabriel to the patriarch Abraham, and preserved at Mecca. The patriarch had perhaps asked the archangel for bread.

CABBAGE, *n.* A familiar kitchen-garden vegetable about as large and wise as a man's head.

The cabbage is so called from Cabagius, a prince who on ascending the throne issued a decree appointing a High Council of Empire, consisting of the members of his predecessor's Ministry and the cabbages in the royal garden. When any of His Majesty's measures of state policy miscarried conspicuously it was gravely announced that several members of the High Council had been beheaded, and his murmuring subjects were appeased.

CACKLE, *v. i.* To celebrate the birth of an egg.

They say that hens do cackle loudest when
  There 's nothing vital in the egg they 've laid;
  And there are hens, professing to have made
A study of mankind, who say that men
Whose business is to drive the tongue or pen
  Make the most clamorous fanfaronade
  O'er their most worthless work; and I 'm afraid
In this respect they 're really like the hen.
Lo! the drum-major in his coat of gold,
  His blazing breeches and high-towering cap,
Imperiously pompous, "bloody, bold
  And resolute"—an awe-inspiring chap!
Who 'd think this gorgeous hero's only virtue
Is that in battle he will never hurt you?

G. J.

CALAMITY, *n.* A more than commonly plain and unmistakable reminder that the affairs of this life are not of our own ordering. Calamities are of two kinds: misfortune to ourselves, and good fortune to others.

CALLOUS, *adj.* Gifted with great fortitude to bear the evils afflicting another.

When Zeno was told that one of his enemies was no more he was observed to be deeply moved. "What!" said one of his disciples, "you weep at the death of an enemy?" "Ah, 't is true," replied the great Stoic; "but you should see me smile at the death of a friend."

CALUMNUS, *n.* A graduate of the School for Scandal.

CAMEL, *n.* A quadruped (the *Splaypes humpidorsus*) of great value to the show business. There are two kinds of camels — the camel proper and the camel improper. It is the latter that is always exhibited.

CANNIBAL, *n.* A gastronome of the old school who preserves the simple tastes and adheres to the natural diet of the pre-pork period.

The practice of cannibalism was once universal, as the smallest knowledge of philology will serve to show. "Oblige us," says the erudite author of the *Delectatio Demonorum*, "by considering the derivation of the word 'sarcophagus,' and see if it be not suggestive of potted meats. Observe the significance of the phrase 'sweet sixteen.' What a world of meaning lurks in the expression 'she's as sweet as a peach,' and how suggestive of luncheon are the words 'tender youth!' A kiss is but a modified bite, and a fond mother, when she rapturously avers that her babe is 'almost good enough to eat,' merely shows that she is herself only a trifle too good to eat it."

CANNON, *n.* An instrument employed in the rectification of national boundaries.

CANONICALS, *n.* The motley worn by Jesters at the Court of Heaven.

CAPITAL, *n.* The seat of misgovernment. That which provides the fire, the pot, the dinner, the table and the knife and fork for the anarchist. The part of the repast that himself supplies is the disgrace before meat. *Capital punishment*, a penalty regarding the justice and expediency of which many worthy persons — including all the assassins — entertain grave misgivings.

CARMELITE, *n.* A mendicant friar of the order of Mt. Carmel.

As Death was a-riding out one day,
Across Mount Carmel he took his way,
  Where he met a mendicant monk,
  Some three or four quarters drunk,
With a holy leer and a pious grin,
Ragged and fat and as saucy as sin,
  Who held out his hands and cried:
"Give, give in Charity's name, I pray.
Give in the name of the Church. O give,
Give that her holy sons may live!"
  And Death replied,
  Smiling long and wide:
  "I'll give, holy father, I'll give thee —
    a ride."

With a rattle and bang
Of his bones, he sprang
From his famous Pale Horse, with his spear;
By the neck and the foot
Seized the fellow, and put
Him astride with his face to the rear.

The Monarch laughed loud with a sound that fell
Like clods on the coffin's empty shell:
"Ho, ho! A beggar on horseback, they say,
Will ride to the devil!" —and *thump*
Fell the flat of his dart on the rump
Of the charger, which galloped away.

Faster and faster and faster it flew,
Till the rocks, and the flocks, and the trees that grew
By the road, were dim, and blended, and blue
To the wild, wide eyes
Of the rider—in size
Resembling a couple of blackberry pies.
Death laughed again, as a tomb might laugh
At a burial service spoiled,
And the mourners' intentions foiled
By the body erecting
Its head and objecting
To further proceedings in its behalf.

Many a year and many a day
Have passed since these events away.
The monk has long been a dusty corse,
And Death has never recovered his horse.

For the friar got hold of its tail,
And steered it within the pale
Of the monastery gray,
Where the beast was stabled and fed,
With barley, and oil, and bread,
Till fatter it grew than the fattest friar,
And so in due course was appointed Prior.

G. J.

CARNIVOROUS, *adj.* Addicted to the cruelty of devouring the timorous vegetarian, his heirs and assigns.

CARTESIAN, *adj.* Relating to Descartes, a famous philosopher, author of the celebrated dictum, *Cogito, ergo sum*—whereby he was pleased to suppose he demonstrated the reality of human existence. The dictum might be improved, however, thus: *Cogito cogito, ergo cogito sum*—"I think that I think, therefore I think that I am;" as close an approach to certainty as any philosopher has yet made.

CAT, *n.* A soft, indestructible automaton provided by nature to be kicked when things go wrong in the domestic circle.

> This is a dog,
>   This is a cat,
> This is a frog,
>   This is a rat.
> Run, dog, mew, cat,
> Jump, frog, gnaw, rat.
>
> *Elevenson.*

CAVILER, *n.* A critic of one's own work.

CEMETERY, *n.* An isolated suburban spot where mourners match lies, poets write at a target and stonecutters spell for a wager. The inscriptions following will serve to illustrate the success attained in these Olympian games:

"His virtues were so conspicuous that his enemies, unable to overlook them, denied them, and his friends, to whose loose lives they were a rebuke, represented them as vices. They are here commemorated by his family, who shared them."

"In the earth we here prepare a
Place to lay our little Clara.
— *Thomas M. and Mary Frazer.*
P. S. — Gabriel will raise her."

CENTAUR, *n.* One of a race of persons who lived before the division of labor had been carried to such a pitch of differentiation, and who followed the primitive economic maxim, "Every man his own horse." The best of the lot was Chiron, who to the wisdom and virtues of the horse added the fleetness of man. The scripture story of the head of John the Baptist on a charger shows that pagan myths have somewhat sophisticated sacred history.

CERBERUS, *n.* The watch-dog of Hades, whose duty it was to guard the entrance — against whom or what does not clearly appear. Everybody, sooner or later, had to go there, and nobody wanted to carry off the entrance. Cerberus is known to have had three heads, and some of the poets have credited him with as many as a hundred. Professor Graybill, whose clerkly erudition and profound knowledge of Greek give his opinion great weight, has averaged all the estimates, and makes the number twenty-seven — a judgment that would be entirely conclusive if Professor Graybill had known (*a*) something about dogs, and (*b*) something about arithmetic.

CHILDHOOD, *n.* The period of human life intermediate between the idiocy of infancy and the folly of youth — two removes from the sin of manhood and three from the remorse of age.

CHRISTIAN, *n.* One who believes that the New Testament is a divinely inspired book admirably suited to the spiritual needs of his neighbor. One who follows the teachings of Christ in so far as they are not inconsistent with a life of sin.

I dreamed I stood upon a hill, and, lo!
The godly multitudes walked to and fro
Beneath, in Sabbath garments fitly clad,
With pious mien, appropriately sad,
While all the church bells made a solemn din—
A fire-alarm to those who lived in sin.
Then saw I gazing thoughtfully below,
With tranquil face, upon that holy show
A tall, spare figure in a robe of white,
Whose eyes diffused a melancholy light.
"God keep you, stranger," I exclaimed. "You are
No doubt (your habit shows it) from afar;
And yet I entertain the hope that you,
Like these good people, are a Christian too."
He raised his eyes and with a look so stern
It made me with a thousand blushes burn
Replied — his manner with disdain was spiced:
"What! I a Christian? No, indeed! I 'm Christ."

G. J.

CIRCUS, *n.* A place where horses, ponies, and elephants are permitted to see men, women, and children acting the fool.

CLAIRVOYANT, *n.* A person, commonly a woman, who has the power of seeing that which is invisible to her patron — namely, that he is a blockhead.

CLARIONET, *n.* An instrument of torture operated by a person with cotton in his ears. There are two instruments that are worse than a clarionet — two clarionets.

CLERGYMAN, *n.* A man who undertakes the management of our spiritual affairs as a method of bettering his temporal ones.

CLIO, *n.* One of the nine Muses. Clio's function was to preside over history — which she did with great dignity, many of the prominent citizens of Athens occupying seats on the platform, the meetings being addressed by Messrs. Xenophon, Herodotus and other popular speakers.

CLOCK, *n.* A machine of great moral value to man, allaying his concern for the future by reminding him what a lot of time remains to him.

A busy man complained one day:
"I get no time!" "What 's that you say?"
Cried out his friend, a lazy quiz;
"You have, sir, all the time there is.
There 's plenty, too, and don't you doubt it —
We 're never for an hour without it."

Purzil Crofe.

CLOSE-FISTED, *adj.* Unduly desirous of keeping that which many deserving persons wish to obtain.

"Close-fisted Scotchman!" Johnson cried
To thrifty J. Macpherson;
"See me — I 'm ready to divide
With any worthy person."

Said Jamie: "That is very true —
The boast requires no backing;
And all are worthy, sir, to you,
Who have what you are lacking."

Anita M. Bobe.

CŒNOBITE, or **CENOBITE,** *n.* A man who piously shuts himself up to meditate upon the sin of wickedness; and to keep it fresh in his mind joins a brotherhood of awful examples.

O cœnobite, O cœnobite,
  Monastical gregarian,
You differ from the anchorite,
  That solitudinarian:
With vollied prayers you wound Old Nick;
With dropping shots he makes him sick.

Quincy Giles.

COMFORT, *n.* A state of mind produced by the contemplation of our neighbor's uneasiness.

COMMENDATION, *n.* The tribute that we pay to achievements that resemble, but do not equal, our own.

COMMERCE, *n.* A kind of transaction in which A plunders from B the goods of C, and for compensation B picks the pocket of D of money belonging to E.

COMMONWEALTH, *n.* An administrative entity operated by an incalculable multitude of political parasites, logically active, but fortuitously efficient.

This commonwealth's capitol's corridors view,
So thronged with a hungry and indolent crew
Of clerks, pages, porters and all attachés
Whom rascals appoint and the populace pays
That a cat cannot slip through the thicket of shins
Nor hear its own shriek for the noise of their chins.
On clerks and on pages, and porters, and all,
Misfortune attend and disaster befall!
May life be to them a succession of hurts;
May fleas by the bushel inhabit their shirts;
May aches and diseases encamp in their bones,
Their lungs full of tubercles, bladders of stones;
May microbes, bacilli, their tissues infest,
And tapeworms securely their bowels digest;
May corn-cobs be snared without hope in their hair,
And frequent impalement their pleasure impair.
Disturbed be their dreams by the awful discourse
Of menacing dressers, sepulchrally hoarse,
By chairs acrobatic and wavering floors—
The mattress that kicks and the pillow that snores!
Sons of cupidity, cradled in sin!
Their criminal ranks may the death angel thin,
Avenging the friend whom I could n't work in.

K. Q.

COMPROMISE, *n.* Such an adjustment of conflicting interests as gives each adversary the satisfaction of thinking he has got what he ought not to have, and is deprived of nothing except what was justly his due.

COMPULSION, *n.* The eloquence of power.

CONDOLE, *v. i.* To show that bereavement is a smaller evil than sympathy.

CONFIDANT, CONFIDANTE, *n.* One entrusted by A with the secrets of B confided to himself by C.

CONGRATULATION, *n.* The civility of envy.

CONGRESS, *n.* A body of men who meet to repeal laws.

CONNOISSEUR, *n.* A specialist who knows everything about something and nothing about anything else.

An old wine-bibber having been smashed in a railway collision, some wine was poured upon his lips to revive him. "Pauillac, 1873," he murmured and died.

CONSERVATIVE, *n.* A statesman who is enamored of existing evils, as distinguished from the Liberal, who wishes to replace them with others.

CONSOLATION, *n.* The knowledge that a better man is more unfortunate than yourself.

CONSUL, *n.* In American politics, a person who having failed to secure an office from the people is given one by the Administration on condition that he leave the country.

CONSULT, *v. t.* To seek another's approval to a course already decided on.

CONTEMPT, *n.* The feeling of a prudent man for an enemy who is too formidable safely to be opposed.

CONTROVERSY, *n.* A battle in which spittle or ink replaces the injurious cannon-ball and the inconsiderate bayonet.

In controversy with the facile tongue —
That bloodless warfare of the old and young —
So seek your adversary to engage
That on himself he shall exhaust his rage,
And, like a snake that 's fastened to the ground,
With his own fangs inflict the fatal wound.
You ask me how this miracle is done?
Adopt his own opinions, one by one,
And taunt him to refute them ; in his wrath
He 'll sweep them pitilessly from his path.
Advance then gently all you wish to prove,
Each proposition prefaced with, "As you 've
So well remarked," or, "As you wisely say,
And I cannot dispute," or, "By the way,
This view of it which, better far expressed,
Runs through your argument." Then leave
the rest
To him, secure that he 'll perform his trust
And prove your views intelligent and just.

Conmore Apel Brune.

CONVENT, *n.* A place of retirement for women who wish for leisure to meditate upon the sin of idleness.

CONVERSATION, *n.* A fair for the display of the minor mental commodities, each exhibitor being too intent upon the arrangement of his own wares to observe those of his neighbor.

CORONATION, *n.* The ceremony of investing a sovereign with the outward and visible signs of his divine right to be blown skyhigh with a dynamite bomb.

CORPORAL, *n.* A man who occupies the lowest rung of the military ladder.

Fiercely the battle raged and, sad to tell,
Our corporal heroically fell!
Fame from her height looked down upon the brawl
And said: "He had n't very far to fall."

Giacomo Smith.

CORPORATION, *n.* An ingenious device for securing individual profit without individual responsibility.

CORSAIR, *n.* A politician of the seas.

COURT FOOL, *n.* The plaintiff.

COWARD, *n.* One who in a perilous emergency thinks with his legs.

CRAFT, *n.* A fool's substitute for brains.

CRAYFISH, *n.* A small crustacean very much resembling the lobster, but less indigestible.

In this small fish I take it that human wisdom is admirably figured and symbolized; for whereas the crayfish doth move only backward, and can have only retrospection, seeing naught but the perils already passed, so the wisdom of man doth not enable him to avoid the follies that beset his course, but only to apprehend their nature afterward.—*Sir James Merivale.*

CREDITOR, *n.* One of a tribe of savages dwelling beyond the Financial Straits and dreaded for their desolating incursions.

CREMONA, *n.* A high-priced violin made in Connecticut.

CRITIC, *n.* A person who boasts himself hard to please because nobody has ever tried to please him.

> There is a land of pure delight,
>   Beyond the Jordan's flood,
> Where saints, apparelled all in white,
>   Fling back the critic's mud.
>
> And as he legs it through the skies,
>   His pelt a sable hue,
> He sorrows sore to recognize
>   The missiles that he threw.
>
> *G. J.*

CROSS, *n.* An ancient religious symbol erroneously supposed to owe its significance to the most solemn event in the history of Christianity, but really antedating it by thousands of years. By many it has been believed to be identical with the *crux ansata* of the ancient phallic worship, but it has been traced even beyond all that we know of that, to the rites of primitive peoples. We have to-day the White Cross as a symbol of chastity, and the Red Cross as a badge of benevolent neutrality in war. Having in mind the former, the reverend Father Gassalasca Jape smites the lyre to the effect following:

"Be good, be good!" the sisterhood
  Cry out in holy chorus;
And, to dissuade from sin, parade
  Their various charms before us.

But why, O why, has ne'er an eye
  Seen her of winsome manner
And youthful grace and pretty face
  Flaunting the White Cross banner?

Now where's the need of speech and screed
  To better our behaving?
A simpler plan for saving man
  (But, first, is he worth saving?)

Is, dears, when he declines to flee
  From bad thoughts that beset him,
Ignores the Law as 't were a straw,
  And wants to sin — don't let him.

CUI BONO? [Latin] What good would that do *me?*

CUNNING, *n.* The faculty that distinguishes a weak animal or person from a strong one. It brings its possessor much mental satisfaction and great material adversity. An Italian proverb says: "The furrier gets the skins of more foxes than asses."

CUPID, *n.* The so-called god of love. This bastard creation of a barbarous fancy was no doubt inflicted upon mythology for the sins of its deities. Of all unbeautiful and inappropriate conceptions this is the most reasonless and offensive. The notion of symbolizing sexual love by a semi-sexless babe, and comparing the pains of passion to the wounds of an arrow — of introducing this pudgy homunculus into art grossly to materialize the subtle spirit and suggestion of the work — this is eminently worthy of the age that, giving it birth, laid it on the doorstep of posterity.

CURIOSITY, *n.* An objectionable quality of the female mind. The desire to know whether or not a woman is cursed with curiosity is one of the most active and insatiable passions of the masculine soul.

CURSE, *v. t.* Energetically to belabor with a verbal slap-stick. This is an operation which in literature, particularly in the drama, is commonly fatal to the victim. Nevertheless, the liability to a cursing is a risk that cuts but a small figure in fixing the rates of life insurance.

CYNIC, *n.* A blackguard whose faulty vision sees things as they are, not as they ought to be. Hence the custom among the Scythians of plucking out a cynic's eyes to improve his vision.

D

DAMN, *int.* A word formerly much used by the Paphlagonians, the meaning of which is lost. By the learned Dr. Dolabelly Gak it is believed to have been a term of satisfaction, implying the highest possible degree of mental tranquillity. Professor Groke, on the other hand, thinks it expressed an emotion of tumultuous delight, because it so frequently occurs in combination with the word *jod* or *god*, meaning "joy." It would be with great diffidence that I should advance an opinion conflicting with that of either of these formidable authorities.

DANCE, *v. i.* To leap about to the sound of tittering music, preferably with arms about your neighbor's wife or daughter. There are many kinds of dances, but all those requiring the participation of the two sexes have two characteristics in common: they are conspicuously innocent, and warmly loved by the guilty.

DANGER, *n.*

A savage beast which, when it sleeps,
  Man girds at and despises,
But takes himself away by leaps
  And bounds when it arises.

Ambat Delaso.

DARING, *n.* One of the most conspicuous qualities of a man in security.

DATARY, *n.* A high ecclesiastical official of the Roman Catholic Church, whose important function is to brand the Pope's bulls with the words *Datum Romæ*. He enjoys a princely revenue and the friendship of God.

DAWN, *n.* The time when men of reason go to bed. Certain old men prefer to rise at about that time, taking a cold bath and a long walk, with an empty stomach, and otherwise mortifying the flesh. They then point with pride to these practices as the cause of their sturdy health and ripe years; the truth being that they are hearty and old, not because of their habits, but in spite of them. The reason we find only robust persons doing this thing is that it has killed all the others who have tried it.

DAY, *n.* A period of twenty-four hours, mostly misspent. This period is divided into two parts, the day proper and the night, or day improper — the former devoted to sins of business, the latter consecrated to the other sort. These two kinds of social activity overlap.

DEAD, *adj.*

> Done with the work of breathing; done
> With all the world; the mad race run
> Through to the end; the golden goal
> Attained and found to be a hole!
>
> *Squatol Johnes.*

DEBAUCHEE, *n.* One who has so earnestly pursued pleasure that he has had the misfortune to overtake it.

DEBT, *n.* An ingenious substitute for the chain and whip of the slave-driver.

As, pent in an aquarium, the troutlet
Swims round and round his tank to find an outlet,
Pressing his nose against the glass that holds him,
Nor ever sees the prison that enfolds him;
So the poor debtor, seeing naught around him,
Yet feels the limits pitiless that bound him;
Grieves at his debt and studies to evade it,
And finds at last he might as well have paid it.

Barlow S. Vode.

DECALOGUE, *n.* A series of commandments, ten in number — just enough to permit an intelligent selection for observance, but not enough to embarrass the choice. Following is the revised edition of the Decalogue, calculated for this meridian.

Thou shalt no God but me adore:
'T were too expensive to have more.

No images nor idols make
For Robert Ingersoll to break.

Take not God's name in vain; select
A time when it will have effect.

Work not on Sabbath days at all,
But go to see the teams play ball.

Honor thy parents. That creates
For life insurance lower rates.

Kill not, abet not those who kill;
Thou shalt not pay thy butcher's bill.

Kiss not thy neighbor's wife, unless
Thine own thy neighbor doth caress.

Don't steal; thou 'lt never thus compete
Successfully in business. Cheat.

Bear not false witness — that is low —
But "hear 't is rumored so and so."

Covet thou naught that thou hast not
By hook or crook, or somehow, got.

G. J.

DECIDE, *v. i.* To succumb to the preponderance of one set of influences over another set.

A leaf was riven from a tree,
"I mean to fall to earth," said he.

The west wind, rising, made him veer.
"Eastward," said he, "I mean to steer."

The east wind rose with greater force.
Said he: "'T were wise to change my course."

With equal power they contend.
He said: "My judgment I suspend."

Down died the winds; the leaf, elate,
Cried: "I 've decided to fall straight."

"First thoughts are best"? That 's not the moral;
Just choose your own and we 'll not quarrel.

Howe'er your choice may chance to fall,
You 've had no hand in it at all.

G. J.

DEFAME, *v. t.* To lie about another. To tell the truth about another.

DEFENCELESS, *adj.* Unable to attack.

DEGENERATE, *adj.* Less conspicuously admirable than one's ancestors. The contemporaries of Homer were striking examples of degeneracy; it required ten of them to raise a rock or a riot that one of the heroes of the Trojan war could have raised with ease. Homer never tires of sneering at the "men who live in these degenerate days," which is perhaps why they suffered him to beg his bread — a marked instance of returning good for evil, by the way, for if they had forbidden him he would certainly have starved.

DEGRADATION, *n.* One of the stages of moral and social progress from private station to political preferment.

DEINOTHERIUM, *n.* An extinct pachyderm that flourished when the Pterodactyl was in fashion. The latter was a native of Ireland, its name being pronounced Terry Dactyl or Peter O'Dactyl, as the man pronouncing it may chance to have heard it spoken or seen it printed.

DEJEUNER, *n.* The breakfast of an American who has been in Paris. Variously pronounced.

DELEGATION, *n.* In American politics, an article of merchandise that comes in sets.

DELIBERATION, *n.* The act of examining one's bread to determine which side it is buttered on.

DELUGE, *n.* A notable first experiment in baptism which washed away the sins (and sinners) of the world.

DELUSION, *n.* The father of a most respectable family, comprising Enthusiasm, Affection, Self-denial, Faith, Hope, Charity, and many other goodly sons and daughters.

All hail, Delusion! Were it not for thee
The world turned topsy-turvy we should see;
For Vice, respectable with cleanly fancies,
Would fly abandoned Virtue's gross advances.

Mumfrey Mappel.

DENTIST, *n.* A prestidigitator who, putting metal into your mouth, pulls coins out of your pocket.

DEPENDENT, *adj.* Reliant upon another's generosity for the support which you are not in a position to exact from his fears.

DEPUTY, *n.* A male relative of an officer-holder or of his bondsman. The deputy is commonly a beautiful young man, with a red necktie and an intricate system of cobwebs extending from his nose to his desk. When accidentally struck by the janitor's broom, he gives off a cloud of dust.

"Chief Deputy," the master cried,
"To-day the books are to be tried
By experts and accountants who
Have been commissioned to go through
Our office here, to see if we
Have stolen injudiciously.
Please have the proper entries made,
The proper balances displayed,

Conforming to the whole amount
Of cash on hand — which they will count.
I 've long admired your punctual way —
Here at the break and close of day,
Confronting in your chair the crowd
Of business men, whose voices loud
And gestures violent you quell
By some mysterious, calm spell—
Some magic lurking in your look
That brings the noisiest to book
And spreads a holy and profound
Tranquillity o'er all around.
So orderly all 's done that they
Who came to draw remain to pay.
But now the time demands, at last,
That you employ your genius vast
In energies more active. Rise
And shake the lightnings from your eyes;
Inspire your underlings, and fling
Your spirit into everything!"
The master hand here dealt a whack
Upon the Deputy's bent back,
When straightway to the floor there fell
A shrunken globe, a rattling shell,
A blackened, withered, eyeless head!
The man had been a twelvemonth dead.

Jamrach Holobom.

DESTINY, *n.* A tyrant's authority for crime and a fool's excuse for failure.

DIAGNOSIS, *n.* A physician's forecast of disease by the patient's pulse and purse.

DIAPHRAGM, *n.* A muscular partition separating disorders of the chest from disorders of the bowels.

DIARY, *n.* A daily record of that part of one's life, which he can relate to himself without blushing.

Sam kept a diary wherein were writ
So many noble deeds and so much wit
That the Recording Angel, when Sam died,
Erased all entries of his own and cried:
"I'll judge you by your diary." Said Sam:
"Thank you; 't will show you what a saint I am"—
Straightway producing, jubilant and proud,
That record from a pocket in his shroud.
The Angel slowly turned the pages o'er,
Each lying line of which he knew before,
Glooming and gleaming as by turns he hit
On noble action and amusing wit;
Then gravely closed the book and gave it back.
"My friend, you 've wandered from your proper track;
You 'd never be content this side the tomb—
For deeds of greatness Heaven has little room,
And Hell 's no latitude for making mirth,"
He said, and kicked the fellow back to earth.

"*The Mad Philosopher*."

DICTATOR, *n.* The chief of a nation that prefers the pestilence of despotism to the plague of anarchy.

DICTIONARY, *n.* A malevolent literary device for cramping the growth of a language and making it hard and inelastic. This dictionary, however, is a most useful work.

DIE, *n.* The singular of "dice." We seldom hear the word, because there is a prohibitory proverb, "Never say die." At long intervals, however, some one says: "The die is cast," which is not true, for it is cut. The word is found in an immortal couplet by that eminent poet and domestic economist, Senator Depew:

> A cube of cheese no larger than a die
> May bait the trap to catch a nibbling mie.

DIGESTION, *n.* The conversion of victuals into virtues. When the process is imperfect, vices are evolved instead —a circumstance from which that wicked writer, Dr. Jeremiah Blenn, infers that the ladies are the greater sufferers from dyspepsia.

DIPLOMACY, *n.* The patriotic art of lying for one's country.

DISABUSE, *v. t.* To present your neighbor with another and better error than the one which he has deemed it advantageous to embrace.

DISCRIMINATE, *v. i.* To note the particulars in which one person or thing is, if possible, more objectionable than another.

DISCUSSION, *n.* A method of confirming others in their errors.

DISOBEDIENCE, *n.* The silver lining to the cloud of servitude.

DISOBEY, *v. t.* To celebrate with an appropriate ceremony the maturity of a command.

His right to govern me is clear as day,
My duty manifest to disobey;
And if that fit observance e'er I shun
May I and duty be alike undone.

Israfel Brown.

DISSEMBLE, *v. i.* To put a clean shirt upon the character.

Let us dissemble. — *Adam.*

DISTANCE, *n.* The only thing that the rich are willing for the poor to call theirs, and keep.

DISTRESS, *n.* A disease incurred by exposure to the prosperity of a friend.

DIVINATION, *n.* The art of nosing out the occult. Divination is of as many kinds as there are fruit-bearing varieties of the flowering dunce and the early fool.

DOG, *n.* A kind of additional or subsidiary Deity designed to catch the overflow and surplus of the world's worship. This Divine Being in some of his smaller and silkier incarnations takes, in the affection of Woman, the place to which there is no human male aspirant. The Dog is a survival — an anachronism. He toils not, neither does he spin, yet Solomon in all his glory never lay upon a door-mat all day long, sun-soaked and fly-fed and fat, while his master worked for the means wherewith to purchase an idle wag of the Solomonic tail, seasoned with a look of tolerant recognition.

DRAGOON, *n.* A soldier who combines steadiness and dash in so equal measure that he makes his advances on foot and his retreats on horseback.

DRAMATIST, *n.* One who adapts plays from the French.

DRUIDS, *n.* Priests and ministers of an ancient Celtic religion which did not disdain to employ the humble allurement of human sacrifice. Very little is now known about the Druids and their faith. Pliny says their religion, originating in Britain, spread eastward as far as Persia. Cæsar says those who desired to study its mysteries went to Britain. Cæsar himself went to Britain, but does not appear to have obtained any high preferment in the Druidical Church, although his talent for human sacrifice was considerable.

Druids performed their religious rites in groves, and knew nothing of church mortgages and the season-ticket system of pew rents. They were, in short, heathens and—as they were once complacently catalogued by a distinguished prelate of the Church of England—"Dissenters."

DUCK-BILL, *n.* Your account at your restaurant during the canvass-back season.

DUEL, *n.* A formal ceremony preliminary to the reconciliation of two enemies. Great skill is necessary to its satisfactory observance; if awkwardly performed the most unexpected and deplorable consequences sometimes ensue. A long time ago a man lost his life in a duel.

That dueling 's a gentlemanly vice
  I hold; and wish that it had been my lot
  To live my life out in some favored spot —
Some country where it is considered nice
To split a rival like a fish, or slice
  A husband like a spud, or with a shot
  Bring down a debtor doubled in a knot
And ready to be put upon the ice.
Some miscreants there are, whom I do long
  To shoot, or stab, or some such way reclaim
The scurvy rogues to better lives and manners.
I seem to see them now — a mighty throng.
  It looks as if to challenge *me* they came,
Jauntily marching with brass bands and banners!

Xamba Q. Dar.

DULLARD, *n.* A member of the reigning dynasty in letters and life. The Dullards came in with Adam, and being both numerous and sturdy have overrun the habitable world. The secret of their power is their insensibility to blows; tickle them with a bludgeon and they laugh with a platitude. The Dullards came originally from Bœotia, whence they were driven by stress of starvation, their dulness having blighted the crops. For some centuries they infested Philistia, and many of them are called Philistines to this day. In the turbulent times of the Crusades they withdrew thence and gradually overspread all Europe, occupying most of the high places in politics, art, literature, science, and theology. Since a detachment of Dullards came over with the Pilgrims in the *May-flower* and made a favorable report of the country, their increase by birth, immigration, and conversion has been rapid and steady. According to the most trustworthy statistics the number of adult Dullards in the United States is but little short of thirty millions, including the statisticians. The intellectual centre of the race is somewhere about Peoria, Illinois, but the New England Dullard is the most impenitently moral.

DUTY, *n.* That which sternly impels us in the direction of profit, along the line of desire.

Sir Lavender Portwine, in favor at court,
Was wroth at his master, who 'd kissed Lady Port.
His anger provoked him to take the king's head,
But duty prevailed, and he took the king's bread,
Instead.

G. J.

E

EAT, *v. i.* To perform successively (and successfully) the functions of mastication, humectation, and deglutition — in short, to eat.

"I was in the drawing-room, enjoying my dinner," said Brillat-Savarin, beginning an anecdote. "What!" interrupted Rochebriant; "eating dinner in a drawing-room?"

"I must beg you to observe, Monsieur," explained the great gastronome, "that I did not say I was eating my dinner, but enjoying it. I had dined an hour before."

EAVESDROP, *v. i.* Secretly to overhear a catalogue of the crimes and vices of another or yourself.

A lady with one of her ears applied
To an open keyhole heard, inside,
Two female gossips in converse free —
The subject engaging them was she.
"I think," said one, "and my husband thinks
That she 's a prying, inquisitive minx!"
As soon as no more of it she could hear
The lady, indignant, removed her ear.
"I will not stay," she said, with a pout,
"To hear my character lied about!"

Gopete Sherany.

ECCENTRICITY, *n.* A method of distinction so cheap that fools employ it to accentuate their incapacity.

ECONOMY, *n.* Purchasing the barrel of whiskey that you do not need for the price of the cow that you cannot afford.

EDIBLE, *adj.* Good to eat, and wholesome to digest, as a worm to a toad, a toad to a snake, a snake to a pig, a pig to a man, and a man to a worm.

EDITOR, *n.* A person who combines the judicial functions of Minos, Rhadamanthus and Æacus, but is placable with an obolus; a severely virtuous censor, but so charitable withal that he tolerates the virtues of others and the vices of himself; who flings about him the splintering lightning and sturdy thunders of admonition till he resembles a bunch of firecrackers petulantly uttering its mind at the tail of a dog; then straightway murmurs a mild, melodious lay, soft as the cooing of a donkey intoning its prayer to the evening star. Master of mysteries and lord of law, high-pinnacled upon the throne of thought, his face suffused with the dim splendors of the Transfiguration, his legs intertwisted and his tongue a-cheek, the editor spills his will along the paper and cuts it off in lengths to suit. And at intervals from behind the veil of the temple is heard the voice of the foreman demanding three inches of wit and six lines of religious meditation, or bidding him turn off the wisdom and whack up some pathos.

O, the Lord of Law on the Throne of Thought,
  A gilded impostor is he.
Of shreds and patches his robes are wrought,
          His crown is brass,
          Himself is an ass,
  And his power is fiddle-dee-dee.
Prankily, crankily prating of naught,
Silly old quilly old Monarch of Thought.
  Public opinion's camp-follower he,
  Thundering, blundering, plundering free.
              Affected,
                    Ungracious,
              Detected,
                    Mendacious,
Respected contemporaree!

J. H. Bumbleshook.

EDUCATION, *n*. That which discloses to the wise and disguises from the foolish their lack of understanding.

EFFECT, *n*. The second of two phenomena which always occur together in the same order. The first, called a Cause, is said to generate the other — which is no more sensible than it would be for one who has never seen a dog except in pursuit of a rabbit to declare the rabbit the cause of the dog.

EGOTIST, *n*. A person of low taste, more interested in himself than in me.

Megaceph, chosen to serve the State
In the halls of legislative debate,
One day with all his credentials came
To the capitol's door and announced his name.
The doorkeeper looked, with a comical twist
Of the face, at the eminent egotist,
And said: "Go away, for we settle here
All manner of questions, knotty and queer,
And we cannot have, when the speaker demands
To be told how every member stands,
A man who to all things under the sky
Assents by eternally voting 'I'."

EJECTION, *n.* An approved remedy for the disease of garrulity. It is also much used in cases of extreme poverty.

ELECTOR, *n.* One who enjoys the sacred privilege of voting for the man of another man's choice.

ELECTRICITY, *n.* The power that causes all natural phenomena not known to be caused by something else. It is the same thing as lightning, and its famous attempt to strike Dr. Franklin is one of the most picturesque incidents in that great and good man's career. The memory of Dr. Franklin is justly held in great reverence, particularly in France, where a waxen effigy of him was recently on exhibition, bearing the following touching account of his life and services to science:

"Monsieur Franqulin, inventor of electricity. This illustrious savant, after having made several voyages around the world, died on the Sandwich Islands and was devoured by savages, of whom not a single fragment was ever recovered."

Electricity seems destined to play a most important part in the arts and industries. The question of its economical application to some purposes is still unsettled, but experiment has already proved that it will propel a street car better than a gas jet and give more light than a horse.

ELEGY, *n.* A composition in verse, in which, without employing any of the methods of humor, the writer aims to produce in the reader's mind the dampest kind of dejection. The most famous English example begins somewhat like this:

The cur foretells the knell of parting day;
  The loafing herd winds slowly o'er the lea;
The wise man homeward plods; I only stay
  To fiddle-faddle in a minor key.

ELOQUENCE, *n.* The art of orally persuading fools that white is the color that it appears to be. It includes the gift of making any color appear white.

ELYSIUM, *n.* An imaginary delightful country which the ancients foolishly believed to be inhabited by the spirits of the good. This ridiculous and mischievous fable was swept off the face of the earth by the early Christians — may their souls be happy in Heaven!

EMANCIPATION, *n.* A bondsman's change from the tyranny of another to the despotism of himself.

He was a slave: at word he went and came;
    His iron collar cut him to the bone.
Then Liberty erased his owner's name,
    Tightened the rivets and inscribed his own.

G. J.

EMBALM, *v. t.* To cheat vegetation by locking up the gases upon which it feeds. By embalming their dead and thereby deranging the natural balance between animal and vegetable life, the Egyptians made their once fertile and populous country barren and incapable of supporting more than a meagre crew. The modern metallic burial casket is a step in the same direction, and many a dead man who ought now to be ornamenting his neighbor's lawn as a tree, or enriching his table as a bunch of radishes, is doomed to a long inutility. We shall get him after awhile if we are spared, but in the meantime the violet and rose are languishing for a nibble at his *glutæus maximus*.

EMOTION, *n.* A prostrating disease caused by a determination of the heart to the head. It is sometimes accompanied by a copious discharge of hydrated chloride of sodium from the eyes.

ENCOMIAST, *n.* A special (but not particular) kind of liar.

END, *n.* The position furthest removed on either hand from the Interlocutor.

The man was perishing apace
  Who played the tambourine:
The seal of death was on his face —
  'T was pallid, for 't was clean.

"This is the end," the sick man said
  In faint and failing tones.
A moment later he was dead,
  And Tambourine was Bones.

Tinley Roquot.

ENOUGH, *pro.* All there is in the world if you like it.

Enough is as good as a feast — for that matter
Enougher 's as good as a feast and the platter.

Arbely C. Strunk.

ENTERTAINMENT, *n.* Any kind of amusement whose inroads stop short of death by dejection.

ENTHUSIASM, *n.* A distemper of youth, curable by small doses of repentance in connection with outward applications of experience. Byron, who recovered long enough to call it "entuzy-muzy," had a relapse which carried him off—to Missolonghi.

ENVELOPE, *n.* The coffin of a document; the scabbard of a bill; the husk of a remittance; the bed-gown of a love-letter.

ENVY, *n.* Emulation adapted to the meanest capacity.

EPAULET, *n.* An ornamented badge, serving to distinguish a military officer from the enemy—that is to say, from the officer of lower rank to whom his death would give promotion.

EPICURE, *n.* An opponent of Epicurus, an abstemious philosopher who, holding that pleasure should be the chief aim of man, wasted no time in gratification of the senses.

EPIGRAM, *n.* A short, sharp saying in prose or verse, frequently characterized by acidity or acerbity and sometimes by wisdom. Following are some of the more notable epigrams of the learned and ingenious Dr. Jamrach Holobom:

We know better the needs of ourselves than of others. To serve oneself is economy of administration.

In each human heart are a tiger, a pig, an ass, and a nightingale. Diversity of character is due to their unequal activity.

There are three sexes: males, females, and girls.

Beauty in women and distinction in men are alike in this: they seem to the unthinking a kind of credibility.

Women in love are less ashamed than men. They have less to be ashamed of.

While your friend holds you affectionately by both your hands you are safe, for you can watch both his.

Woman would be more charming if one could fall into her arms without falling into her hands.

Think not to atone for wealth by apology: you must make restitution by a loan to the accuser.

Study good women and ignore the rest,
For he best knows the sex who knows the best.

Before undergoing a surgical operation arrange your temporal affairs. You may live.

Intolerance is natural and logical, for in every dissenting opinion lies an assumption of superior wisdom.

"Who art thou?" said Saint Peter at the Gate.

"I am known as Memory."

"What presumption! — go back to Hell. And who, perspiring friend, art thou?"

"My name is Satan. I am looking for —"

"Take your penal apparatus and be off."

And Satan, laying hold of Memory, said: "Come along, you scoundrel; you make happiness wherever you are not."

Self-denial is the weak indulgence of a propensity to forego.

Men talk of selecting a wife; horses of selecting an owner.

You are not permitted to kill a woman that has injured you, but nothing forbids you to reflect that she is growing older every minute. You are avenged 1440 times a day.

A sweetheart is a bottle of wine. A wife is a wine bottle.

He gets on best with women who best knows how to get on without them.

"Who am I?" asked an awakened soul. "That is the only knowledge that is denied to you here," answered a smiling angel. "This is Heaven."

Woman's courage is ignorance of danger; man's is hope of escape.

Women of genius commonly have masculine faces, figures, and manners. In transplanting brains to an alien soil God leaves a little of the original earth clinging to the roots.

The heels of Detection are sore from the toes of Remorse.

Twice we see Paradise. In youth we name it Life; in age, Youth.

There are but ten Commandments, true,
But that 's no hardship, friend, to you;
The unmentioned sins that tax your wit
You 're not commanded to commit.

Fear of the darkness is more than an inherited superstition — it is at night, mostly, that the king thinks.

A chain is only as strong as its weakest link, but a multitude is as wise as its wisest member if it obeys him.

"Who art thou?" said Mercy.
"Revenge, the father of Justice."
"Thou wearest thy son's clothing."
"One must be clad."
"Farewell — I go to attend thy son."
"Thou wilt find him hiding in yonder jungle."

When God had finished this terrestrial frame
And all things else, with or without a name,
The nothing that remained within his hand
Said: "Make me into something fine and grand,
Thine angels to amuse and entertain."
God heard and made it into human brain.

If you wish to slay your enemy make haste, O make haste, for already Nature's knife is at his throat and yours.

To most persons a sense of obligation is insupportable; beware upon whom you inflict it.

Bear me, good oceans, to some isle
 Where I may never fear
The snake alurk in woman's smile,
 The tiger in her tear.
Yet bear not with me one, O deeps,
Who never smiles and never weeps.

The ninety-and-nine who most loudly demand opportunity most bitterly revile the one who has made good use of it.

Life and Death threw dice for a child.

"I win!" cried Life.

"True," said Death, "but you need a nimbler tongue to proclaim your luck. The child is already dead of age."

How blind is he who, powerless to discern
The glories that about his pathway burn,
Walks unaware the avenues of Dream,
Nor sees the domes of Paradise agleam!
O Golden Age, to him more nobly planned
Thy light lies ever upon sea and land.
From sordid scenes he lifts his soul at will,
And sees a Grecian god on every hill!

In childhood we expect, in youth demand, in manhood hope, and in age beseech.

EPITAPH, *n.* An inscription on a tomb, showing that virtues acquired by death have a retroactive effect. Following is a touching example:

Here lie the bones of Parson Platt,
Wise, pious, humble, and all that,
Who showed us life as all should live it;
Let that be said — and God forgive it!

ERUDITION, *n.* Dust shaken out of a book into an empty skull.

So wide his erudition's mighty span,
He knew by heart the laws of God and man,
And only came by accident to grief —
He thought, poor man, 't was right to be a thief.

Romach Pute.

ESOPHAGUS, *n.* That part of the alimentary canal that lies between pleasure and business.

ESOTERIC, *adj.* Very particularly abstruse and consummately occult. The ancient philosophies were of two kinds, — *exoteric*, those that the philosophers themselves could partly understand, and *esoteric*, those that nobody could understand. It is the latter that have most profoundly affected modern thought and found greatest acceptance in our time.

ESSENTIAL, *adj.* Pertaining to the *essence*, or that which determines the distinctive character of a thing. Persons who, because they do not know the English language, are driven to the unprofitable vocation of writing for American newspapers, commonly use this word in the sense of *necessary*, as, "April rains are *essential* to June harvests."

ETHNOLOGY, *n.* The science that treats of the various tribes of Man, as robbers, thieves, swindlers, dunces, lunatics, idiots, and ethnologists.

EUCHARIST, *n.* A sacred feast of the religious sect of Theophagi.

A dispute once unhappily arose among the members of this sect as to what it was that they ate. In this controversy some five hundred thousand have already been slain, and the question is still unsettled.

EULOGY, *n.* Praise of a person who has either the advantages of wealth and power, or the consideration to be dead.

EVANGELIST, *n.* A bearer of good tidings, particularly (in a religious sense) such as assure us of our own salvation, and the damnation of our neighbors.

EVERLASTING, *adj.* Lasting forever. It is with no small diffidence that I venture to offer this brief and elementary definition, for I am not unaware of the existence of a bulky volume by the Rt. Rev. Dr. Sprowle, sometime Bishop of Worcester, entitled, *A Partial Definition of the Word "Everlasting," as Used in the Authorized Version of the Holy Scriptures.* His book was once esteemed of great authority in the Anglican Church, and is still, I understand, studied with pleasure to the mind and profit to the soul.

EXCEPTION, *n.* A thing which takes the liberty to differ from other things of its class, as an honest man, a truthful woman, etc. "The exception proves the rule" is an expression constantly upon the lips of the ignorant, who parrot it from one another with never a thought of its absurdity. In the Latin, "*Exceptio probat regulam*" means that the exception *tests* the rule, puts it to the proof, not *confirms* meaning from this excellent dictum and substituted a contrary one of his own, exerted an evil power which appears to be immortal.

EXCESS, *n.* In morals, an indulgence that enforces by appropriate penalties the law of moderation.

Hail high Excess!—especially in wine.
  To thee in worship do I bend the knee
  Who preach abstemiousness unto me —
My skull thy pulpit, as my paunch thy shrine.
Precept on precept, aye, and line on line,
  Could ne'er persuade so sweetly to agree
  With reason as thy touch, exact and free,
Upon my forehead and along my spine.
At thy command eschewing pleasure's cup,
  With the hot grape I warm no more my wit;
  When on thy stool of penitence I sit
I 'm quite converted, for I can't get up.
Ungrateful he who afterward would falter
To make new sacrifices at thine altar!

EXCOMMUNICATION, *n.*

This "excommunication" is a word
In speech ecclesiastical oft heard,
And means the damning, with bell, book, and candle,
Some sinner whose opinions are a scandal—

A rite permitting Satan to enslave him
Forever, and forbidding Christ to save him.
Gat Huckle.

EXECUTIVE, *n.* An officer of the Government whose duty it is to enforce the wishes of the legislative power until such time as the judicial department shall be pleased to pronounce them mischievous and of no effect. Following is an extract from an old book entitled, *The Lunarian Astonished* —Pfeiffer & Co., Boston, 1803:

"LUNARIAN: Then when your Congress has passed a law it goes directly to the Supreme Court in order that it may at once be known whether it is constitutional.

"TERRESTRIAN: O no; it does not require the approval of the Supreme Court until having perhaps been enforced for many years somebody objects to its operation against himself — I mean his client. The President, if he approves it, begins to execute it at once.

"LUNARIAN: Then the executive power is a part of the legislative. Do your policemen also have to approve the local ordinances that they enforce?

"TERRESTRIAN: Not yet — at least not in their capacity of constables. Generally speaking though, all laws require the approval of those whom they are intended to restrain.

"LUNARIAN: Ah, I see. The death warrant is not valid until signed by the murderer.

"TERRESTRIAN: My friend, you put it too strongly; we are not so consistent.

"LUNARIAN: But this system of maintaining an expensive judicial machinery to pass upon the validity of laws only after they have long been executed, and then only when brought before the court by some private person — does it not cause great confusion?

"TERRESTRIAN: It does.

"LUNARIAN: Why then should not your laws, previously to being executed, be validated, not by the signature of your President, but by that of the Chief Justice of the Supreme Court?

"TERRESTRIAN: There is no precedent for any such course.

"LUNARIAN: Precedent? What is that?

"TERRESTRIAN: It has been defined by five hundred lawyers in three volumes each. So how can any one know?"

EXHORT, *v. t.* In religious affairs, to put the conscience of another upon the spit and roast it to a nut-brown discomfort.

EXILE, *n.* One who serves his country by residing abroad, yet is not an ambassador.

An English sea-captain being asked if he had read "The Exile of Erin," replied: "No, sir, but I should like to anchor on it." Years afterward, when he had been hanged as a pirate after a career of unparalleled atrocities, the following memorandum was found in the ship's log that he had kept at the time of his reply:

"Aug. 3d, 1842. Made a joke on the ex-Isle of Erin. Coldly received. War with the whole world!"

EXISTENCE, *n.*

A transient, horrible, fantastic dream,
Wherein is nothing yet all things do seem;
From which we 're wakened by a friendly nudge
Of our bedfellow Death, and cry: "O fudge!"

EXPERIENCE, *n.* The wisdom that enables us to recognize as an undesirable old acquaintance the folly that we have already embraced.

To one who, journeying through night and fog,
Is mired waist deep in an unwholesome bog,
Experience, like the rising of the dawn,
Shows him the path he never should have gone.

Joel Frad Bink.

EXPOSTULATION, *n.* One of the many methods by which fools prefer to lose their friends.

EXTINCTION, *n.* The raw material out of which theology created the future state.

F

FAIRY, *n.* A creature, variously fashioned and endowed, that formerly inhabited the meadows and forests. It was nocturnal in its habits, and somewhat addicted to dancing and theft of children. The fairies are now believed by naturalists to be extinct, though a clergyman of the Church of England saw three near Colchester as lately as 1855, while passing through a park after dining with the lord of the manor. The sight greatly staggered him, and he was so affected that his account of it was incoherent. In the year 1807 a troop of fairies visited a wood near Aix and carried off the daughter of a peasant, who had been seen to enter it with a bundle of clothing. The son of a wealthy *bourgeois* disappeared about the same time, but afterward returned. He had seen the abduction and been in pursuit of the fairies. Justinian Gaux, a writer of the fourteenth century, avers that so great is the fairies' power of transformation that he saw one change itself into two opposing armies and fight a battle with great slaughter, and that the next day, after it had resumed its original shape and gone away, there were seven hundred bodies of the slain which the villagers had to bury. He does not say if any of the wounded recovered. In the time of Henry III, of England, a law was made which prescribed the death penalty for "Kyllynge, wowndynge, or mamynge" a fairy, and it was universally respected.

FAITH, *n.* Belief without evidence in what is told by one who speaks without knowledge of things without parallel.

FAMOUS, *adj.* Conspicuously miserable.

Done to a turn on the iron, behold
  Him who to be famous aspired.
Content? Well, his grill has a plating of gold,
  And his twistings are greatly admired.

Hassan Brubuddy.

FASHION, *n.* A deity whom the wise ridicule, yet the discreet obey.

A king there was who lost an eye
  In some excess of passion;
And straight his courtiers all did try
  To follow the new fashion.

Each dropped one eyelid when before
  The throne he ventured, thinking
'T would please the king. That monarch swore
  He 'd slay them all for winking.

What should they do? They were not hot
  To hazard such disaster;
They dared not close an eye — dared not
  See better than their master.

Seeing them lacrymose and glum,
  A leech consoled the weepers:
He spread small rags with liquid gum
  And covered half their peepers.

The court all wore the stuff, the flame
  Of royal anger dying.
That 's how court-plaster got its name
  Unless I 'm greatly lying.

Naramy Oof.

FEAST, *n.* A festival. A religious celebration signalized by gluttony and drunkenness, frequently in honor of some holy person distinguished for abstemiousness. In the Roman Catholic Church feasts are "movable" and "immovable," but the celebrants are uniformly immovable until they are full. In their earliest development these entertainments took the form of feasts for the dead; such were held by the Greeks, under the name of *Nemeseia*, by the Aztecs and Peruvians, as in modern times they are popular with the Chinese; though it is believed that the ancient dead, like the modern, were light eaters. Feasts *on* the dead are celebrated with great *éclat* in Fiji. Among the many feasts of the Romans was the *Novemdiale*, which was held, according to Livy, whenever stones fell from heaven. Of all the feast days of the various Christian churches none has any sanction in the gospel. Men make gods of their bellies, and then these gods ordain festivals.

FELON, *n.* A person of greater enterprise than discretion, who in embracing an opportunity has formed an unfortunate attachment.

FEMALE, *n*. One of the opposing, or unfair, sex.

The Maker, at Creation's birth,
With living things had stocked the earth.
From elephants to bats and snails,
They all were good, for all were males.
But when the Devil came and saw
He said: "By Thine eternal law
Of growth, maturity, decay,
These all must quickly pass away
And leave untenanted the earth
Unless Thou dost establish birth" —
Then tucked his head beneath his wing
To laugh — he had no sleeve — the thing
With deviltry did so accord,
That he'd suggested to the Lord.
The Master pondered this advice,
Then shook and threw the fateful dice
Wherewith all matters here below
Are ordered, and observed the throw;
Then bent His head in awful state,
Confirming the decree of Fate.
From every part of earth anew
The conscious dust consenting flew,
While rivers from their courses rolled
To make it plastic for the mould.
Enough collected (but no more,
For niggard Nature hoards her store)
He kneaded it to flexile clay,
While Nick unseen threw some away.
And then the various forms He cast,

Gross organs first and fine the last;
No one at once evolved, but all
By even touches grew and small
Degrees advanced, till, shade by shade,
To match all living things, He 'd made
Females, complete in all their parts
Except (His clay gave out) the hearts.
"No matter," Satan cried; "with speed
I 'll fetch the very hearts they need" —
So flew to Hell and soon brought back
The number needed, in a sack.
That night earth rang with sounds of strife —
Ten million males had each a wife;
That night sweet Peace her pinions spread
O'er Hell — ten million devils dead!

G. J.

FIB, *n.* A lie that has not cut its teeth. An habitual liar's nearest approach to truth: the perigee of his eccentric orbit.

When David said: "All men are liars," Dave,
Himself a liar, fibbed like any thief.
Perhaps he thought to weaken disbelief
By proof that even himself was not a slave
To Truth; though I suspect the aged knave
Had been of all her servitors the chief
Had he but known a fig's reluctant leaf
Is more than e'er she wore on land or wave.
No, David served not the Naked Truth when he

Struck that sledge-hammer blow at all his race;
Nor did he hit the nail upon the head:
For reason shows that it could never be,
And the facts contradict him to his face.
Men are not liars all, for some are dead.

Bartle Quinker.

FICKLENESS, *n.* The iterated satiety of an enterprising affection.

FIDDLE, *n.* An instrument to tickle human ears by friction of a horse's tail on the entrails of a cat.

To Rome said Nero: "If to smoke you turn
I shall not cease to fiddle while you burn."
To Nero Rome replied: "Pray do your worst,
'T is my excuse that you were fiddling first."

Orm Pludge.

FIDELITY, *n.* A virtue peculiar to those who are about to be betrayed.

FINANCE, *n.* The art or science of managing revenues and resources for the best advantage of the manager. The pronunciation of this word with the i long and the accent on the first syllable is one of America's most precious discoveries and possessions.

FLAG, *n*. A colored rag borne above troops and hoisted on forts and ships. It appears to serve the same purpose as certain signs that one sees on vacant lots in London — "Rubbish may be shot here."

FLESH, *n*. The Second Person of the secular Trinity.

FLOP, *v*. Suddenly to change one's opinions and go over to another party. The most notable flop on record was that of Saul of Tarsus, who has been severely criticised by some of our partisan journals.

FLY-SPECK, *n*. The prototype of punctuation. It is observed by Garvinus that the systems of punctuation in use by the various literary nations depended originally upon the social habits and general diet of the flies infesting the several countries. These creatures, which have always been distinguished for a neighborly and companionable familiarity with authors, liberally or niggardly embellish the manuscripts in process of growth under the pen, according to their bodily habit, bringing out the sense of the work by a species of interpretation superior to, and independent of, the writer's powers. The "old masters" of literature — that is to say, the early writers whose work is so esteemed by later scribes and critics in the same language — never punctuated at all, but worked right along free-handed, without that abruption of the thought which comes from the use of points. (We observe the same thing in children to-day, whose usage in this particular is a striking and beautiful instance of the law that the infancy of individuals reproduces the methods and stages of development characterizing the infancy of races.) In the work of these primitive scribes all the punctuation is found, by the modern investigator with his optical instruments and chemical tests, to have been inserted by the writers' ingenious and serviceable collaborator, the common house-fly—*Musca maledicta.* In transcribing these ancient MSS, for the purpose either of making the work their own or preserving what they naturally regard as divine revelations, later writers reverently and accurately copy whatever marks they find upon the papyrus or parchment, to the unspeakable enhancement of the lucidity of the thought and value of the work. Writers contemporary with the copyists naturally avail themselves of the obvious advantages of these marks in their own work, and with such assistance as the flies of their own household may be willing to grant, frequently rival and sometimes surpass the older compositions, in respect at least of punctuation, which is no small glory. Fully to understand the important services that flies perform to literature it is only necessary to lay a page of some popular novelist alongside a saucer of cream-and-molassess in a sunny room and observe "how the wit brightens and the style refines" in accurate proportion to the duration of exposure.

FOLLY, *n.* That "gift and faculty divine" whose creative and controlling energy inspires Man's mind, guides his actions, and adorns his life.

Folly ! although Erasmus praised thee once
  In a thick volume, and all authors known,
  If not thy glory yet thy power have shown,
Deign to take homage from thy son who hunts
Through all thy maze his brothers, fool and dunce,
  Their lives to mend and to sustain his own,
  However feebly be his arrows thrown,
Howe'er each hide the flying weapon blunts.

All-Father Folly! be it mine to raise,
  With lusty lung, here on this western strand
  With all thine offspring thronged from every land,
Thyself inspiring me, the song of praise.
And if too weak, I 'll hire, to help me bawl,
Dick Watson Gilder, gravest of us all.

Aramis Loto Frope.

FOOL, *n.* A person who pervades the domain of intellectual speculation and diffuses himself through the channels of moral activity. He is omnific, omniform, omnipercipient, omniscient, omnipotent. He it was who invented letters, printing, the railroad, the steamboat, the telegraph, the platitude, and the circle of the sciences. He created patriotism and taught the nations war — founded theology, philosophy, law, medicine, and San Francisco. He established monarchical and republican government. He is from everlasting to everlasting — such as creation's dawn beheld he fooleth now. In the morning of time he sang upon primitive hills, and in the noonday of existence headed the procession of being. His grandmotherly hand has warmly tucked-in the set sun of civilization, and in the twilight he prepares Man's evening meal of milk-and-morality and turns down the covers of the universal grave. And after the rest of us shall have retired for the night of eternal oblivion, he will sit up to write a history of human civilization.

FORCE, *n.*

" Force is but might," the teacher said —
" That definition 's just."
The boy said naught but thought instead,
Remembering his pounded head:
" Force is not might but must ! "

FOREFINGER, *n.* The finger commonly used in pointing out two malefactors.

FOREORDINATION, *n.* This looks like an easy word to define, but when I consider that pious and learned theologians have spent long lives in explaining it, and written libraries to explain their explanations; when I remember that nations have been divided and bloody battles caused by the difference between foreordination and predestination, and that millions of treasure have been expended in the effort to prove and disprove its compatibility with freedom of the will and the efficacy of prayer, praise, and a religious life, — recalling these awful facts in the history of the word, I stand appalled before the mighty problem of its signification, abase my spiritual eyes, fearing to contemplate its portentous magnitude, reverently uncover and humbly refer it to His Eminence Cardinal Gibbons and His Grace Bishop Potter.

FORGETFULNESS, *n.* A gift of God bestowed upon debtors in compensation for their destitution of conscience.

FORK, *n.* An instrument used chiefly for the purpose of putting dead animals into the mouth. Formerly the knife was employed for this purpose, and by many worthy persons is still thought to have many advantages over the other tool, which, however, they do not altogether reject, but use to assist in charging the knife. The immunity of these persons from swift and awful death is one of the most striking proofs of God's mercy to those that hate Him.

FORMA PAUPERIS [Latin]. In the character of a poor person — a method by which a litigant without money for lawyers is considerately permitted to lose his case.

When Adam long ago in Cupid's awful court
  (For Cupid ruled ere Adam was invented)
Sued for Eve's favor, says an ancient law report,
  He stood and pleaded unhabilimented.

"You sue *in formâ pauperis*, I see," Eve cried;
  "Actions can't here be that way prosecuted."
So all poor Adam's motions coldly were denied:
  He went away — as he had come — nonsuited.

G. J.

FRANKALMOIGNE, *n.* The tenure by which a religious corporation holds lands on condition of praying for the soul of the donor. In mediæval times many of the wealthiest fraternities obtained their estates in this simple and cheap manner, and once when Henry VIII of England sent an officer to confiscate certain vast possessions which a fraternity of monks held by frankalmoigne, "What!" said the Prior, "would your master stay our benefactor's soul in Purgatory?" "Ay," said the officer, coldly, "an ye will not pray him thence for naught he must e'en roast." "But look you, my son," persisted the good man, "this act hath rank as robbery of God!" "Nay, nay, good father, my master the king doth but deliver Him from the manifold temptations of too great wealth."

FREEBOOTER, *n.* A conqueror in a small way of business, whose annexations lack the sanctifying merit of magnitude.

FREEDOM, *n.* Exemption from the stress of authority in a beggarly half dozen of restraint's infinite multitude of methods. A political condition that every nation supposes itself to enjoy in practical monopoly. Liberty. The distinction between freedom and liberty is not accurately known; naturalists have never been able to find a living specimen of either.

Freedom, as every schoolboy knows,
  Once shrieked as Kosciusko fell;
On every wind, indeed, that blows
    I hear her yell.

She screams whenever monarchs meet,
  And parliaments as well,
To bind the chains about her feet
    And toll her knell.

And when the sovereign people cast
  The votes they cannot spell,
Upon the lung-impested blast
    Her clamors swell.

For all to whom the power 's given
To sway or to compel,
Among themselves apportion heaven
And give her hell.

Blary O'Gary.

FREEMASONS, *n.* An order with secret rites, grotesque ceremonies, and fantastic costumes, which, originating in the reign of Charles II, among working artisans of London, has been joined successively by the dead of past centuries in unbroken retrogression until now it embraces all the generations of man on the hither side of Adam and is drumming up distinguished recruits among the pre-Creational inhabitants of Chaos and the Formless Void. The order was founded at different times by Charlemagne, Julius Cæsar, Cyrus, Solomon, Zoroaster, Confucius, Thothmes, and Buddha. Its emblems and symbols have been found in the Catacombs of Paris and Rome, on the stones of the Parthenon and the Chinese Great

Wall, among the temples of Karnak and Palmyra and in the Egyptian Pyramids — always by a Freemason.

FRIENDLESS, *adj.* Having no favors to bestow. Destitute of fortune. Addicted to utterance of truth and common sense.

FRIENDSHIP, *n.* A ship big enough to carry two in fair weather, but none in foul.

> The sea was calm and the sky was blue;
> Merrily, merrily sailed we two.
>   (High barometer maketh glad.)
> On the tipsy ship, with a dreadful shout,
> The tempest descended and we fell out.
>   (O the walking is nasty bad!)
>
> *Armit Huff Bettle.*

FROG, *n.* An amphibious reptile with edible kickers. When young, this creature is called a Marywog or Thaddeuspole, and as such maintains a tail, subsequently eschewed. The first mention of frogs in profane literature is in Homer's narrative of the war between them and the mice. Skeptical persons have doubted Homer's authorship of the work, but the learned, ingenious, and industrious Dr. Schliemann has set the question forever at rest by uncovering the bones of the slain frogs. One of the forms of moral suasion by which Pharaoh was lobbied in favor of the Israelities was a plague of frogs, but Pharaoh, who liked them *fricasée*, remarked, with truly oriental stoicism, that he could stand it as long as the frogs and the Jews could; so the programme was changed. The frog is a diligent songster, having a good voice but no ear. The libretto of his favorite opera, as written by Aristophanes, is brief, simple, and effective — "brekekex-koäx"; the music is apparently by that eminent composer, Richard Wagner. Horses have a frog in each hoof — a thoughtful provision of nature, enabling them to jump.

FRYING-PAN, *n.* One part of the penal apparatus employed in that hell-upon-earth, a woman's kitchen. The frying-pan was invented by Calvin, and by him used in scrambling span-long infants that had died without baptism; but observing one day the horrible torment of a tramp who had incautiously pulled a fried babe from the waste-dump and devoured it, it occurred to the great divine to rob death of its terrors by introducing the frying-pan into every household in Geneva. Thence it spread to all corners of the world, and has been of invaluable assistance in the propagation of his sombre faith. The following lines (said to be from the pen of His Grace Bishop Potter) seem to imply that the usefulness of this utensil is not limited to this world; but as the consequences of its employment in this life reach over into the life to come, so also itself may be found on the other side, rewarding its devotees:

Old Nick was summoned to the skies.
  Said Peter: "Your intentions
Are good, but you lack enterprise
  Concerning new inventions.

"Now, broiling is an ancient plan
  Of torment, but I hear it
Reported that the frying-pan
  Sears best the wicked spirit.

"Go get one — fill it up with fat —
  Fry sinners brown and good in 't."
"I know a trick worth two o' that,"
  Said Nick — "I 'll cook their food in 't."

FUNERAL, *n.* A pageant whereby we attest our respect for the dead by enriching the undertaker, and strengthen our grief by an expenditure that deepens our groans and doubles our tears.

The savage dies — they sacrifice a horse
To bear to happy hunting-grounds the corse.
Our friends expire — we make the money fly
In hope their souls will chase it through the sky.

Jex Wopley.

FUTURE, *n.* That period of time in which our affairs prosper, our friends are true, and our happiness is assured.

G

GALLOWS, *n.* A stage for the performance of miracle plays, in which the leading actor is translated to heaven. In this country the gallows is chiefly remarkable for the number of persons who escape it.

> Whether on the gallows high
> Or where blood flows the reddest,
> The noblest place for man to die —
> Is where he dies the deadest.
>
> *Old Play.*

GARGOYLE, *n.* A rain-spout projecting from the eaves of mediæval buildings, commonly fashioned into a grotesque caricature of some personal enemy of the architect or owner of the building. This was especially the case in churches and ecclesiastical structures generally, in which the gargoyles presented a perfect rogues' gallery of local heretics and controversialists. Sometimes when a new dean and chapter were installed the old gargoyles were removed and others substituted having a closer relation to the private animosities of the new incumbents.

GARTER, *n.* An elastic band intended to keep a woman from coming out of her stockings and desolating the country. An order of merit established by Edward III of England, and conferred upon persons who have distinguished themselves in the royal favor.

GENEROUS, *adj.* Originally this word meant noble by birth and was rightly applied to a great multitude of persons. It now means noble by nature, and is taking a bit of a rest.

GENEALOGY, *n.* An account of one's descent from an ancestor who did not particularly care to trace his own.

GENTEEL, *adj.* Refined, after the fashion of a gent.

Observe with care, my son, the distinction I reveal:
A gentleman is gentle and a gent genteel.
Heed not the definitions your "Unabridged" presents,
For dictionary makers are generally gents.
G. J.

GEOGRAPHER, *n.* A chap who can tell you offhand the difference betweeen the outside of the world and the inside.

Habeam, geographer of wide renown,
Native of Abu-Keber's ancient town,
In passing thence along the river Zam
To the adjacent village of Xelam,
Bewildered by the multitude of roads,
Got lost, lived long on migratory toads,
Then from exposure miserably died,
And grateful travellers bewailed their guide.
Henry Haukhorn.

GEOLOGY, *n.* The science of the earth's crust — to which, doubtless, will be added that of its interior whenever a man shall come up garrulous out of a well. The geological formations of the globe already noted are catalogued thus: The Primary, or lower one, consists of rocks, bones of mired mules, gas-pipes, miners' tools, antique statues minus the nose, Spanish doubloons, and ancestors. The Secondary is largely made up of red worms and moles. The Tertiary comprises railway tracks, patent pavements, grass, snakes, mouldy boots, beer bottles, tomato cans, intoxicated citizens, garbage, anarchists, snap-dogs, and fools.

GHOST, *n.* The outward and visible sign of an inward fear.

> He saw a ghost.
> It occupied — that dismal thing! —
> The path that he was following.
> Before he 'd time to stop and fly,
> An earthquake trifled with the eye
> That saw a ghost.

He fell as fall the early good;
Unmoved that awful spectre stood.
The stars that danced before his ken
He wildly brushed away, and then
He saw a post.
Jared Macphester.

Accounting for the uncommon behavior of ghosts, Heine mentions somebody's ingenious theory to the effect that they are as much afraid of us as we of them. Not quite, if I may judge from such tables of comparative speed as I am able to compile from memories of my own experience.

There is one insuperable obstacle to a belief in ghosts. A ghost never comes naked: he appears either in a winding-sheet or "in his habit as he lived." To believe in him, then, is to believe that not only have the dead the power to make themselves visible after there is nothing left of them, but that the same extraordinary gift inheres in textile fabrics. Supposing the products of the loom to have this ability, what object would they have in exercising it? And why does not the apparition of a suit of clothes sometimes walk abroad without a ghost in it? These be riddles of significance. They reach away down and get a convulsive grasp on the very tap-root of this flourishing faith.

GHOUL, *n.* A demon addicted to the reprehensible habit of devouring the dead. The existence of ghouls has been disputed by that class of controversialists who are more concerned to deprive the world of comforting beliefs than give it anything good in their place, but nobody now seriously denies it. In 1640 Father Seechi saw one in a cemetery near Florence and frightened it away with the sign of the cross. He describes it as gifted with several heads and an uncommon allowance of limbs, and he saw it in more than one place at a time. The good man was coming away from dinner at the time and explains that if he had not been "heavy with eating" he would have seized the demon at all hazards. Atholston relates that a ghoul was caught by some sturdy peasants in a churchyard at Sudbury and ducked in a horsepond. (He appears to think that so distinguished a criminal should have been ducked in a tank of rose-water.) The water turned at once to blood "and so contynues unto ys daye." The pond has since been bled with a ditch. As late as the beginning of the last century a ghoul was cornered in the crypt of the cathedral at Amiens and the whole population surrounded the place. Twenty armed men with a priest at their head, bearing a crucifix, entered and captured the ghoul, which, thinking to escape by the stratagem, had transformed itself to the semblance of a well-known citizen, but was nevertheless hanged, drawn and quartered in the midst of hideous popular orgies. The citizen whose shape the demon had assumed was so affected by the sinister occurrence that he never again showed himself in Amiens and his fate remains a mystery.

GLUTTON, *n.* A person who escapes the evils of moderation by committing dyspepsia.

GNOME, *n.* In North-European mythology, a dwarfish imp inhabiting the interior parts of the earth and having special custody of mineral treasures. Bjorsen, who died in 1765, says gnomes were common enough in the southern parts of Sweden in his boyhood, and he frequently saw them scampering on the hills in the evening twilight. Ludwig Binkerhoof saw three as recently as 1792, in the Black Forest, and Sneddeker avers that in 1803 they drove a party of miners out of a Silesian mine. Basing our computations upon data supplied by these statements, we find that the gnomes probably became extinct about 1640.

GNOSTICS, *n.* A sect of philosophers who tried to engineer a fusion between the early Christians and the Platonists. The former would not go into the caucus and the combination failed, greatly to the chagrin of the fusion managers.

GNU, *n.* An animal of South Africa, which in its domesticated state resembles a horse, a buffalo, and a stag. In its wild condition it is something like a thunderbolt, an earthquake, and a cyclone.

A hunter from Kew caught a distant view
  Of a peacefully meditative gnu,
And he said: "I'll pursue, and my hands imbrue
  In its blood at a closer interview."
But that beast did ensue and the hunter it threw
  O'er the top of a palm that adjacent grew;
And he said as he flew: "It is well I withdrew
  Ere, losing my temper, I wickedly slew
  That really meritorious gnu."

Jarn Leffer.

GOOD, *adj.* Sensible, madam, to the worth of this present writer. Alive, sir, to the advantages of letting him alone.

GOOSE, *n.* A bird that supplies quills for writing. These, by some occult process of nature, are penetrated and suffused with various degrees of the bird's intellectual energies and emotional character, so that when inked and drawn mechanically across paper by a person called an "author," there results a very fair and accurate transcript of the fowl's thought and feeling. The difference in geese, as discovered by this ingenious method, is considerable: many are found to have only trivial and insignificant powers, but some are seen to be very great geese indeed.

GORGON, *n.*

The Gorgon was a maiden bold
Who turned to stone the Greeks of old

Who looked upon her awful brow.
We dig them out of ruins now,
And swear that workmanship so bad
Proves all the ancient sculptors mad.

GOUT, *n.* A physician's name for the rheumatism of a rich patient.

GRACES, *n.* Three beautiful goddesses, Aglaia, Thalia, and Euphrosyne, who attended upon Venus, serving without salary. They were at no expense for board and clothing, for they ate nothing to speak of and dressed according to the weather, wearing whatever breeze happened to be blowing.

GRAMMAR, *n.* A system of pitfalls thoughtfully prepared for the feet of the self-made man, along the path by which he advances upon our understanding.

GRAPE, *n.*

> Hail noble fruit! — by Homer sung,
> Anacreon and Khayyam;
> Thy praise is ever on the tongue
> Of better men than I am.

The lyre my hand has never swept,
  The song I cannot offer:
My humbler service pray accept —
  I 'll help to kill the scoffer.

The water-drinkers and the cranks
  Who load their skins with liquor —
I 'll gladly bare their belly-tanks
  And tap them with my sticker.

Fill up, fill up, for wisdom cools
  When e'er we let the wine rest.
Here 's death to Prohibition's fools
  And every kind of vine-pest!

Jamrach Holobom.

GRAPESHOT, *n.* An argument which the future is preparing in answer to the demands of American Socialism.

GRAVE, *n.* A place in which the dead are laid to await the coming of the medical student.

Beside a lonely grave I stood —
    With brambles 't was encumbered;
The winds were moaning in the wood,
    Unheard by him who slumbered.

A rustic standing near, I said:
  "He cannot hear it blowing!"
"'Course not," said he: "the feller 's dead —
    He can't hear nowt that 's going."

"Too true," I said; "alas, too true—
No sounds his sense can quicken!"
"Well, Mister, wot is that to you?—
The deadster ain't a kickin'."

I knelt and prayed: "O Father smile
On him, and mercy show him!"
That countryman looked on the while,
And said: "Ye did n't know him."

Pobeter Dunk.

GRAVITATION, *n.* The tendency of all bodies to approach one another with a strength proportioned to the quantity of matter they contain—the quantity of matter they contain being ascertained by the strength of their tendency to approach one another. This is a lovely and edifying illustration of how science, having made A the proof of B, makes B the proof of A.

GREAT, *adj.*

"I 'm great," the Lion said—"I reign
The monarch of the wood and plain!"

The Elephant replied: "I 'm great—
No quadruped can match my weight!"

"I 'm great — no animal has half
So long a neck!" said the Giraffe.

"I 'm great," the Kangaroo said — "see
My caudal muscularity!"

The 'Possum said: "I 'm great — behold,
My tail is lithe and bald and cold!"

An Oyster fried was understood
To say: "I 'm great because I 'm good!"

Each reckons greatness to consist
In that in which he heads the list,

And Braywell thinks he tops his class
Because he is the greatest ass.

Arion Spurl Doke.

GUILLOTINE, *n.* A machine which makes a Frenchman shrug his shoulders with good reason.

In his great work on *Divergent Lines of Racial Evolution*, the learned and ingenious Professor Brayfugle argues from the prevalence of this gesture — the shrug — among Frenchmen, that they are descended from turtles, and it is simply a survival of the habit of retracting the head inside the shell. It is with reluctance that I differ with so eminent an authority, but in my judgment (as more elaborately set forth and enforced in my work entitled *Hereditary Emotions* — lib. II, c. XI) the shrug is a poor foundation upon which to build so important a theory, for previously to the Revolution the gesture was unknown. I have not a doubt that it is directly referable to the terror inspired by the guillotine during the period of that instrument's awful activity.

GUNPOWDER, *n.* An agency employed by civilized nations for the settlement of disputes which might become troublesome if left unadjusted. By most writers the invention of gunpowder is ascribed to the Chinese, but not upon very convincing evidence. Milton says it was invented by the devil to kill angels with, and this opinion seems to derive some support from the scarcity of angels. Moreover, it has the hearty concurrence of the Hon. James Wilson, Secretary of Agriculture. Secretary Wilson became interested in gunpowder through an event that occurred on the Government experimental farm in the District of Columbia. One day, some years ago, some rogue, imperfectly reverent of his profound attainments and personal character, presented him with a sack of gunpowder, representing it as the seed of the *Flashawful flabbergastor*, a Patagonian cereal of great commercial value, admirably adapted to this climate. The good Secretary was instructed to spill it along in a furrow and afterward inhume it with soil. This he at once proceeded to do, and had made a continuous line of it all the way across a ten-acre field, when he was made to look backward by a shout from the generous donor, who at once dropped a lighted match into the furrow at the starting-point. Contact with the earth had somewhat dampened the powder, but the startled functionary saw himself pursued by a tall moving pillar of fire and smoke in fierce evolution. He stood for a moment paralyzed and speechless, then he recollected an engagement, and, dropping all, absented himself thence with such surprising celerity that to the eyes of spectators along the route selected he appeared like a long, dim streak of farmer prolonging itself with inconceivable rapidity through seven villages, and audibly refusing to be comforted. "Great Scott! what is that?" cried a surveyor's chainman, shading his eyes and gazing at the fading line of agriculturist which bisected his visible horizon. "That," said the surveyor, carelessly, glancing at the phenomenon and again centring his attention upon his instrument, "is the Meridian of Washington."

H

HABEAS CORPUS. A writ by which a man may be taken out of jail and asked how he likes it.

HABIT, *n.* A shackle for the free.

HADES, *n.* The lower world; the residence of departed spirits; the place where the dead live.

Among the ancients the idea of Hades was not synonymous with our Hell, many of the most respectable men of antiquity residing there in a very comfortable kind of way. Indeed, the Elysian Fields themselves were a part of Hades, though they have since been removed to Paris. When the Jacobean version of the New Testament was in process of evolution the pious and learned men engaged in the work insisted by a majority vote on translating the Greek word "Hades" as "Hell"; but a conscientious minority member secretly possessed himself of the record and struck out the objectionable word wherever he could find it. At the next meeting, the Bishop of Winchester, looking over the work, suddenly sprang to his feet and said with considerable excitement: "Gentlemen, somebody has been razing 'Hell' here!" Years afterwards the good prelate's death was made sweet by the reflection that he had been the means (under Providence) of making an important, serviceable, and immortal addition to the phraseology of the English tongue.

HAG, *n.* An elderly lady whom you do not happen to like; sometimes called, also, a hen, or cat. Old witches, sorceresses, etc., were called hags from the belief that their heads were surrounded by a kind of baleful lumination or nimbus — hag being the popular name of that peculiar electrical light sometimes observed in the hair. At one time hag was not a word of reproach: Drayton speaks of a "beautiful hag, all smiles," much as Shakespeare said, "sweet wench." It would not now be proper to call your sweetheart a hag — that pleasure is reserved for her grandchildren.

HALF, *n.* One of two equal parts into which a thing may be divided, or considered as divided. In the fourteenth century a heated discussion arose among the theologists and philosophers as to whether Omniscience could part an object into three halves; and the pious Father Aldrovinus publicly prayed in the cathedral at Rouen that God would demonstrate the affirmative of the proposition in some signal and unmistakable way, and particularly (if it should please Him) upon the body of that hardy blasphemer, Manutius Procinus, who maintained the negative. Procinus, however, was spared to die of the bite of a viper.

HALO, *n.* Properly, a luminous ring encircling an astronomical body, but not infrequently confounded with "aureola," or "nimbus," a somewhat similar phenomenon worn as a head-dress by divinities and saints. The halo is a purely optical illusion, produced by moisture in the air, in the manner of a rainbow; but the aureola is conferred as a sign of superior sanctity, in the same way as a bishop's mitre, or the Pope's tiara. In the painting of the Nativity, by Szedgkin, a pious artist of Pesth, not only do the Virgin and the Child wear the nimbus, but an ass nibbling hay from the sacred manger is similarly decorated and, to his lasting honor be it said, appears to bear his unaccustomed dignity with a truly saintly grace.

HAND, *n.* A singular instrument worn at the end of the human arm and commonly thrust into somebody's pocket.

HANDKERCHIEF, *n.* A small square of silk or linen, used in various ignoble offices about the face and especially serviceable at funerals to conceal the lack of tears. The handkerchief is of recent invention; our ancestors knew nothing of it and intrusted its duties to the sleeve. Shakespeare's introducing it into the play of "Othello" is an anachronism: Desdamona dried her nose with her coat-tails as Dr. Mary Walker and other reformers have done in our own day—an evidence that revolutions sometimes go backward.

HANGMAN, *n.* An officer of the law charged with duties of the highest dignity and utmost gravity, and held in hereditary disesteem by a populace having a criminal ancestry. In some of the American States his functions are now performed by an electrician, as in New Jersey, where executions by electricity have recently been ordered — the first instance known to this lexicographer of anybody questioning the expediency of hanging Jerseymen.

HAPPINESS, *n.* An agreeble sensation arising from contemplating the misery of another.

HARANGUE, *n.* A speech by an opponent, who is known as an harangoutang.

HARBOR, *n.* A place where ships taking shelter from storms are exposed to the fury of the customs.

HARMONISTS, *n.* A sect of Protestants, now extinct, who came from Europe in the beginning of the last century and were distinguished for the bitterness of their internal controversies and dissensions.

HASH, *x.* There is no definition for this word — nobody knows what hash is.

HATCHET, *n.* A young axe, known among Indians as a Thomashawk.

> " O bury the hatchet, irascible Red,
> For peace is a blessing," the White Man said.
> The Savage concurred, and that weapon interred,
> With imposing rites, in the White Man's head.
>
> *John Lukkus.*

HATRED, *n.* The sentiment appropriate to the occasion of another's success or superiority.

HEAD-MONEY, *n.* A capitation or poll-tax.

In ancient times there lived a king
Whose tax-collectors could not wring
From all his subjects gold enough
To make the royal way less rough.
For pleasure's highway, like the dames
Whose premises adjoin it, claims
Perpetual repairing. So
The tax-collectors in a row
Appeared before the throne to pray
Their master to devise some way
To swell the revenue. "So great,"
Said they, "are the demands of state
A tithe of all that we collect
Will scarcely meet them. Pray reflect:
How, if one-tenth we must resign,
Can we exist on t'other nine?"
The monarch asked them in reply:
"Has it occurred to you to try
The advantage of economy?"
"It has," the spokesman said: "we sold
All of our gay garrotes of gold;
With plated-ware we now compress
The necks of those whom we assess.
Plain iron forceps we employ
To mitigate the miser's joy
Who hoards, with greed that never tires,
That which your Majesty requires."
Deep lines of thought were seen to plow
Their way across the royal brow.
"Your state is desperate, no question;
Pray favor me with a suggestion."
"O King of Men," the spokesman said,

"If you 'll impose upon each head
A tax, the augmented revenue
We 'll cheerfully divide with you."
As flashes of the sun illume
The parted storm-cloud's sullen gloom,
The king smiled grimly. "I decree
That it be so — and, not to be
In generosity outdone,
Declare you, each and every one,
Exempted from the operation
Of this new law of capitation.
But lest the people censure me
Because they 're bound and you are free,
'T were well some clever scheme were laid
By you this poll-tax to evade.
I 'll leave you now while you confer
With my most trusted minister."
The monarch from the throne-room walked
And straightway in among them stalked
A silent man, with brow concealed,
Bare-armed — his gleaming axe revealed!

G. J.

HEARSE, *n.* Death's baby-carriage.

HEART, *n.* An automatic, muscular blood-pump. Figuratively, this useful organ is said to be the seat of emotions and sentiments — a very pretty fancy which, however, is nothing but a survival of a once universal belief. It is now known that the sentiments and emotions reside in the stomach, being evolved from food by chemical action of the gastric fluid. The exact process by which a beefsteak becomes a feeling — tender or not, according to the age of the animal from which it was cut; the successive stages of elaboration through which a caviare sandwich is transmuted to a quaint fancy and reappears as a pungent epigram; the marvellous functional methods of converting a hard-boiled egg into religious contrition, or a cream-puff into a sigh of sensibility — these things have been patiently ascertained by M. Pasteur, and by him expounded with convincing lucidity. (See, also, my monograph on "The Essential Identity of the Spiritual Affections and Certain Intestinal Gases Freed in Digestion" — 4to, 687 pp.) In a scientific work entitled, I believe,

Delectatio Demonorum (John Camden Hotten, London, 1873) this view of the sentiments receives a striking illustration and support in the author's account of an experiment made with a view to testing it. The stomach of a man who had died of a surfeit of turkey on Thanksgiving Day was removed and kept tightly closed until it was greatly distended with the gases produced by digestion. The compression on the neck of it being then relaxed, the words, "Praise God from whom all blessings flow!" were heard with distinct articulation, as the swollen organ collapsed. It is nonsense to ignore, belittle, pervert or deny the significance of a fact like that. For further light upon this subject, consult Professor Dam's famous treatise on "Love as a product of Alimentary Maceration."

HEAT, *n.*

Heat, says Professor Tyndall, is a mode
Of motion, but I know now how he's proving

His point; but this I know — hot words bestowed
With skill will set the human fist a-moving,
And where it stops the stars burn free and wild.
Trust an eye-witness — I've been there, my child.
Gorton Swope.

HEATHEN, *n.* A benighted creature who has the folly to worship something that he can see and feel. According to Professor Howison, of the California State University, Hebrews are heathens.

"The Hebrews are heathens!" says Howison. He 's
A Christian philosopher. I 'm
A scurril agnostical chap, if you please,
Addicted too much to the crime
Of religious discussion in rhyme.

Though Hebrew and Howison cannot agree
On a modus vivendi — not they! —
Yet Heaven has had the designing of me,
And I have n't been built in a way
To joy in the thick of the fray.

For this of my creed is the soul and the gist,
And the truth of it I aver:
Who differs from me in his faith is an 'ist,
An 'ite, an 'ic, and an 'er —
And I 'm down upon him or her!

Let Howison urge with perfunctory chin
  Toleration — that 's all very well,
But a roast is " nuts " to his nostril thin,
  And he 's running — I know by the smell —
  A secret, particular hell!

Bissell Gip.

HEAVEN, *n.* A place where the wicked cease from troubling you with talk of their personal affairs, and the good listen with attention while you expound your own.

HEBREW, *n.* A male Jew, as distinguished from the Shebrew, an altogether superior creation.

HELPMATE, *n.* A wife, or bitter half.

" Now, why is yer wife called a helpmate, Pat? "
  Says the priest. " Since the time o' yer wooin'
She 's niver assisted in what ye were at —
  For it 's naught ye are ever doin'."

" That 's true of yer Riverence," Patrick replies,
  And no sign of contrition evinces;
" But, bedad, it 's a fact which the word implies,
  For she helps to mate the expinses! "

Marley Wottel.

HEMP, *n.* A plant from whose fibrous bark is made an article of neckwear which is frequently put on after public speaking in the open air and prevents the wearer from taking cold.

HERMIT, *n.* A person whose vices and follies are not sociable.

HERS, *pron.* His.

HIBERNATE, *v. n.* To pass the winter season in domestic seclusion. There have been many singular popular notions about the hibernation of various animals. Many believe that the bear hibernates during the whole winter and subsists by mechanically sucking its paws. It is admitted that it comes out of its retirement in the spring so lean that it has to try twice before it can cast a shadow. Three or four centuries ago, in England, no fact was better attested than that swallows passed the winter months in the mud at the bottoms of the brooks, clinging together in globular masses. They have apparently been compelled to give up the custom on account of the foulness of the brooks. Sotus Escobius discovered in Central Asia a whole nation of people who hibernated. By some investigators, the fasting of Lent is supposed to have been originally a modified form of hibernation, to which the Church gave a religious significance; but this view is strenuously opposed by that eminent authority, Bishop Kip, who does not wish any honors denied to the memory of the Founder of his family.

HIPPOGRIFF, *n.* An animal (now extinct) which was half horse and half griffin. The griffin was itself a compound creature, half lion and half eagle. The hippogriff was therefore one quarter eagle, which is two dollars and fifty cents in gold. The study of natural history is full of surprises.

HISTORIAN, *n.* A broad-gauge gossip.

HISTORY, *n.* An account, mostly false, of events, mostly unimportant, which are brought about by rulers, mostly knaves, and soldiers, mostly fools.

Of Roman history, great Niebuhr's shown
'T is nine-tenths lying. Faith, I wish 't were known,
Ere we accept great Niebuhr as a guide,
Wherein he blundered and how much he lied.

Salder Bupp.

HOG, *n.* A bird remarkable for the catholicity of its appetite and serving to illustrate that of ours. Among the Mahometans and Jews, the hog is not in favor as an article of diet, but is respected for the delicacy of its habits, the beauty of its plumage, and the melody of its voice. It is chiefly as a songster that the fowl is esteemed; a cage of him in full chorus has been known to draw tears from two persons at once. The scientific name of this dicky-bird is

Porcus Rockefelleri. Mr. Rockefeller did not discover the hog, but it is considered his by right of resemblance.

HOMŒOPATHIST, *n.* The humorist of the medical profession.

HOMŒOPATHY, *n.* A school of medicine midway between Allopathy and Christian Science. To the last both the others are distinctly inferior, for Christian Science will cure imaginary diseases and they can not.

HOMICIDE, *n.* The slaying of one human being by another. There are four kinds of homicide: felonious, excusable, justifiable, and praiseworthy, but it makes no great difference to the person slain whether he fell by one kind or another — the classification is for advantage of the lawyers.

HOMILETICS, *n.* The science of adapting sermons to the spiritual needs, capacities, and conditions of the congregation.

So skilled the parson was in homiletics
That all his moral purges and emetics
To medicine the spirit were compounded
With a most just discrimination, founded
Upon a rigorous examination
Of tongue and pulse and heart and respiration.
Then, having diagnosed each one's condition,
His scriptural specifics this physician
Administered — his pills so efficacious
And pukes of disposition so vivacious
That souls afflicted with ten kinds of Adam
Were convalescent ere they knew they had 'em.
But Slander's tongue — itself all coated — uttered
Her bilious mind and scandalously muttered
That in the case of patients having money
The pills were sugar and the pukes were honey.

Biography of Bishop Potter.

HONORABLE, *adj.* Afflicted with an impediment in one's reach. In legislative bodies it is customary to mention all members as honorable; as, "the honorable gentleman is a scurvy cur."

HOPE, *n.* Desire and expectation rolled into one.

Delicious Hope! when naught to man is left —
Of fortune destitute, of friends bereft;
When even his dog deserts him, and his goat
With tranquil disaffection chews his coat
While yet it hangs upon his back; then thou,
The star far-flaming on thine angel brow,
Descendest, radiant, from the skies to hint
The promise of a clerkship in the Mint.

Fogarty Weffing.

HOSPITALITY, *n.* The virtue which induces us to lodge and feed certain persons who are not in want of food and lodging.

HOSTILITY, *n.* A peculiarly sharp and specially applied sense of the earth's overpopulation. Hostility is classed as *active* and *passive*; as (respectively) the feeling of a woman for her female friends, and that which she entertains for all the rest of her sex.

HOURI, *n.* A comely female inhabiting the Mohammedan Paradise to make things cheery for the good musselman, whose belief in her existence marks a noble discontent with his earthly spouse, whom he denies a soul. By that good lady the Houris are said to be held in deficient esteem.

HOUSE, *n.* A hollow edifice erected for the habitation of man, rat, mouse, beetle, cockroach, fly, mosquito, flea, bacillus, and microbe. *House of Correction*, a place of reward for political and personal service, and for the detention of appropriations and offenders. *House of God*, a building with a steeple and a mortgage on it. *House-dog*, a pestilent beast kept on domestic premises to insult persons passing by and appal the hardy visitor. *House-maid*, a youngerly person of the opposing sex employed to be variously disagreeable and ingeniously unclean in the station in which it has pleased God to place her.

HOUSELESS, *adj.* Having paid all taxes on household goods.

HOVEL, *n.* The fruit of a flower called the Palace.

Twaddle had a hovel,
  Twiddle had a palace;
Twaddle said: "I 'll grovel
Or he 'll think I bear him malice"—
A sentiment as novel
As a chimney on a chalice.

Down upon the middle
  Of his legs fell Twaddle
And astonished Mr. Twiddle,
  Who began to lift his noddle,
Feed upon the fiddle-
  Faddle flummery, unswaddle
A new-born self-sufficiency and think himself a model.

G. J.

HUMANITY, *n.* The human race, collectively, exclusive of the anthropoid poets.

HUMORIST, *n.* A plague that would have softened down the hoar austerity of Pharaoh's heart and persuaded him to dismiss Israel with his best wishes, cat-quick.

Lo! the poor humorist, whose tortured mind
Sees jokes in crowds, though still to gloom inclined —
Whose simple appetite, untaught to stray,
His brains, renewed by night, consumes by day.
He thinks, admitted to an equal sty,
A graceful hog would bear his company.

Alexander Poke.

HURRICANE, *n.* An atmospheric demonstration once very common but now generally abandoned for the tornado and cyclone. The hurricane is still in popular use in the West Indies and is preferred by certain old-fashioned sea-captains. It is also used in the construction of the upper decks of steamboats, but generally speaking, the hurricane's usefulness has outlasted it.

HURRY, *n.* The dispatch of bunglers.

HUSBAND, *n.* One who, having dined, is charged with the care of the plate.

HYBRID, *n.* A pooled issue.

HYDRA, *n.* A kind of animal that the ancients catalogued under many heads.

HYENA, *n.* A beast held in reverence by some oriental nations from its habit of frequenting at night the burial-places of the dead. But the observant medical student loathes the creature, for he knows why it goes to the graveyard. He has met it there.

HYPOCHONDRIASIS, *n.* Depression of one's own spirits.

Some heaps of trash upon a vacant lot
Where long the village rubbish had been shot
Displayed a sign among the stuff and stumps —
"Hypochondriasis." It meant The Dumps.

Bogul S. Purvy.

HYPOCRITE, *n.* One who, professing virtues that he does not respect, secures the advantage of seeming to be what he despises.

I

I is the first letter of the alphabet, the first word of the language, the first thought of the mind, the first object of affection. In grammar it is a pronoun of the first person and singular number. Its plural is said to be *We*, but how there can be more than one myself is doubtless clearer to the grammarians than it is to the author of this incomparable dictionary. Conception of two myselves is difficult, but fine. The frank yet graceful use of "I" distinguishes a good writer from a bad; the latter carries it with the demeanor of the Impenitent Thief packing his cross up Calvary.

ICHOR, *n.* A fluid that served the gods and goddesses in place of blood.

Fair Venus, speared by Diomed,
Restrained the raging chief and said:
"Behold, rash mortal, whom you 've bled —
Your soul 's stained white with ichorshed!"

Mary Doke.

ICONOCLAST, *n.* A breaker of idols, the worshippers whereof are imperfectly gratified by the performance, and most strenuously protest that he unbuildeth but doth not reëdify, that he teareth down but pileth not up. For the poor things would have other idols in place of those he thwacketh upon the mazzard and dispelleth. But the iconoclast saith: "Ye shall have none at all, for ye need them not; and if the rebuilder fooleth round hereabout, behold I will depress the head of him and sit thereon till he squawk it."

IDIOT, *n.* A member of a large and powerful tribe whose influence in human affairs has always been dominant and controlling. The Idiot's activity is not confined to any special field of thought or action, but "pervades and regulates the whole." He has the last word in everything; his decision is unappealable. He sets the fashions of opinion and taste, dictates the limitations of speech and circumscribes conduct with a dead-line.

IDLENESS, *n.* A model farm where the devil experiments with seeds of new sins and promotes the growth of untried vices.

IGNORAMUS, *n.* A person unacquainted with certain kinds of knowledge familiar to yourself, and having certain other kinds that you know nothing about.

> Dumble was an ignoramus,
> Mumble was for learning famous.
> Mumble said one day to Dumble:
> "Ignorance should be more humble.
> Not a spark have you of knowledge
> That was got in any college."

Dumble said to Mumble: "Truly
You 're self-satisfied unduly.
Of things in college I 'm denied
A knowledge — you of all outside."

Borelli.

ILLUMINATI, *n.* A sect of Spanish heretics of the latter part of the sixteenth century; so called because they were light weights—*cunctationes illuminati.*

ILLUSTRIOUS, *adj.* Suitably placed for the shafts of malice, envy, and detraction.

IMAGINATION, *n.* A warehouse of facts, with poet and liar in joint ownership.

IMBECILITY, *n.* A kind of divine inspiration, or sacred fire, affecting censorious critics of this dictionary.

IMMIGRANT, *n.* An unenlightened person who thinks one country better than another.

IMMODEST, *adj.* Having a strong sense of one's own merit, coupled with a feeble conception of worth in others.

There was once a man in Ispahan
  Ever and ever so long ago,
And he had a head, the phrenologists said,
    That fitted him for a show.

For his modesty's bump was so large a lump
  (Nature, they said, had taken a freak)
That its summit stood far above the wood
    Of his hair, like a mountain peak.

So modest a man in all Ispahan,
  Over and over again they swore —
So humble and meek, you would vainly seek;
    None ever was found before.

Meantime the hump of that awful bump
  Into the heavens contrived to get
To so great a height that they called the wight
    The man with a minaret.

There was n't a man in all Ispahan
  Prouder, or louder in praise of his chump:
With a tireless tongue and a brazen lung
    He bragged of that beautiful bump

Till the Shah in a rage sent a trusty page
  Bearing a sack and a bow-string too,
And that gentle child explained as he smiled:
    "A little present for you."

The saddest man in all Ispahan,
  Sniffed at the gift, yet accepted the same.
"If I 'd lived," said he, "my humility
    Had given me deathless fame!"

Sukker Uffro.

IMMORAL, *adj.* Inexpedient. Whatever in the long run, and with regard to the greater number of instances men find to be generally inexpedient, comes to be considered wrong, wicked, immoral. If men's notions of right and wrong have any other basis than this of expediency; if they originated, or could have originated, in any other way; if actions have in themselves a moral character apart from, and nowise dependent on, their consequences—then all philosophy is a lie and reason a disorder of the mind.

IMMORTALITY, *n.*

A toy which people cry for,
And on their knees apply for,
Dispute, contend, and lie for,
    And if allowed
    Would be right proud
Eternally to die for.

G. J.

IMPALE, *v. t.* In popular usage to pierce with any weapon which remains fixed in the wound. This, however, is inaccurate; to impale is, properly, to put to death by thrusting an upright sharp stake into the body, the victim being left in a sitting position. This was a common mode of punishment among many of the nations of antiquity, and is still in high favor in China and other parts of Asia. Down to the beginning of the Fifteenth Century it was widely employed in churching heretics and schismatics. Wolecraft calls it the "stoole of repentynge," and among the common people it was jocularly known as "riding the one legged horse." Ludwig Salzmann informs us that in Thibet impalement is considered the most appropriate punishment for crimes against religion; and although in China it is sometimes awarded to secular offences, it is most frequently adjudged in cases of sacrilege. To the person in actual experience of impalement it must be a matter of minor importance by what kind of civil or religious dissent he was made acquainted with its discomforts; but doubtless he would feel a certain satisfaction if able to contemplate himself in the character of a weather-cock on the spire of the True Church.

IMPARTIAL, *adj.* Unable to perceive any promise of personal advantage from espousing either side of a controversy or adopting either of two conflicting opinions.

IMPENITENCE, *n.* A state of mind intermediate in point of time between sin and punishment.

IMPIETY, *n.* Your irreverence toward my deity.

IMPOSITION, *n.* The act of blessing or consecrating by the laying on of hands — a ceremony common to many ecclesiastical systems, but performed with the frankest sincerity by the sect known as Thieves.

"Lo! by the laying on of hands,"
  Say parson, priest, and dervise,
"We consecrate your cash and lands
  To ecclesiastic service.
No doubt you 'll swear till all is blue
At such an imposition. Do."

Pollo Doncas.

IMPOSTOR, *n.* A rival aspirant to public honors.

IMPROBABILITY, *n.*

His tale he told with a solemn face
And a tender, melancholy grace.
    Improbable 't was, no doubt,
    When you came to think it out,
    But the fascinated crowd
    Their deep surprise avowed
And all with a single voice averred
'T was the most amazing thing they 'd heard —
All save one who spake never a word,
    But sat as mum
    As if deaf and dumb,
Serene, indifferent, and unstirred.
    Then all the others turned to him
    And scrutinized him limb from limb —

Scanned him alive,
But he seemed to thrive
And tranquiler grow each minute,
As if there were nothing in it.
"What! what!" cried one, "are you not amazed
At what our friend has told?" He raised
Soberly then his eyes and gazed
In a natural way
And proceeded to say,
As he crossed his feet on the mantel-shelf:
"O no — not at all; I'm a liar myself."

IMPROVIDENCE, *n.* Provision for the needs of to-day from the revenues of to-morrow.

IMPUNITY, *n.* Wealth.

INADMISSIBLE, *adj.* Not competent to be considered. Said of certain kinds of testimony which juries are supposed to be unfit to be entrusted with, and which judges, therefore, rule out, even of proceedings before themselves alone. Hearsay evidence is inadmissible because the person quoted was unsworn and is not before the court for examination; yet the most momentous actions, military, political, commercial, and of every other kind, are daily undertaken on hearsay evidence. There is no religion in the world that has any other basis than hearsay evidence. Revelation is hearsay evidence; that the Scriptures are the word of God we have only the testimony of men long dead whose identity is not clearly established and who are not known to have been sworn in any sense. Under the rules of evidence as they now exist in this country, no single assertion in the Bible has in its support any evidence admissible in a court of law. It cannot be proved that the battle of Blenheim ever was fought, that there was such a person as Julius Cæsar, such an empire as Assyria. But as records of courts of justice are admissible, it can easily be proved that powerful and malevolent magicians once existed and were a scourge to mankind. The evidence (including confession) upon which certain women were convicted of witchcraft and executed was without a flaw; it is still absolutely unimpeachable. The judges' decisions based on it were sound in logic and in law. Nothing in any existing court was ever more thoroughly proved than the charges of witchcraft and sorcery for which so many suffered death. If there are no witches, human testimony and human reason are alike destitute of value.

INAUSPICIOUSLY, *adv.* In an unpromising manner, the auspices being unfavorable. Among the Romans it was customary before undertaking any important action or enterprise to obtain from the augurs, or state prophets, some hint of its probable outcome; and one of their favorite and most trustworthy modes of divination consisted in observing the flight of birds — the omens thence derived being called *auspices.* Newspaper reporters and certain miscreant lexicographers have decided that the word — always in the plural — shall mean "patronage" or "management"; as, "The festivities were under the auspices of the Ancient and Honorable Order of Body-Snatchers"; or, "The hilarities were auspicated by the Knights of Hunger."

A Roman slave appeared one day
Before the Augur. "Tell me, pray,
If —" here the Augur, smiling, made
A checking gesture and displayed
His open palm, which plainly itched,
For visibly its surface twitched.
An *obolus* (the Latin nickel)
Successfully allayed the tickle,
And then the slave proceeded: "Please
Inform me whether Fate decrees
Success or failure in what I
To-night (if it be dark) shall try.
Its nature? Never mind — I think
'T is writ on this" — and with a wink
Which darkened half the earth, he drew
Another *obolus* to view,
Its brazen face attentive scanned,
Then slipped it in the good man's hand,

Who with great gravity said: "Wait
While I retire to question Fate."
That holy person then withdrew
His sacred clay and passing through
The temple's rearward gate, cried "Shoo!"
Waving his robe of office. Straight
Each sacred peacock and its mate
(Maintained for Juno's favor) fled
With clamor from the trees o'erhead,
Where they were perching for the night.
The temple's roof received their flight,
For thither they would always go
When danger threatened them below.
Back to the slave the Augur went:
"My son, forecasting the event
By flight of birds, I must confess
The auspices deny success."
That slave retired, a sadder man,
Abandoning his secret plan —
Which was (as well the crafty seer
Had from the first divined) to clear
The wall and fraudulently seize
On Juno's poultry in the trees.

G. J.

INCOME, *n.* The natural and rational gauge and measure of respectability, the commonly accepted standards being artificial, arbitrary, and fallacious; for, as "Sir Sycophas Aureolater" in the play has justly remarked, "the true use and function of property (in whatsoever it consisteth — coins, or land, or houses, or merchant-stuff, or anything which may be named as holden of right to one's own subservience) as also of honors, titles, preferments, and place, and all favor and acquaintance of persons of quality or ableness, are but to get money. Hence it followeth that all things are truly to be rated as of worth in measure of their serviceableness to that end; and their possessors should take rank in agreement thereto, neither the lord of an unproducing manor, howsoever broad and ancient, nor he who bears an unremunerate dignity, nor yet the pauper favorite of a king, being esteemed of level excellency with him whose riches are of daily accretion; and hardly should they whose wealth is barren claim and rightly take more honor than the poor and unworthy."

INCOMPATIBILITY, *n.* In matrimony a similarity of tastes, particularly the taste for domination. Incompatibility may, however, consist of a meek-eyed matron living just around the corner. It has even been known to wear a moustache.

INCOMPOSSIBLE, *adj.* Unable to exist if something else exists. Two things are incompossible when the world of being has scope enough for one of them, but not enough for both — as the poet Gilder and God's mercy to man. Incompossibility, it will be seen, is only incompatibility let loose. Instead of such low language as "Go heel yourself — I mean to kill you on sight," the words, "Sir, we are incompossible," would convey an equally significant intimation, and in stately courtesy are altogether superior.

INCUBUS, *n.* One of a race of highly improper demons who, though probably not wholly extinct, may be said to have seen their best nights. For a complete account of *incubi* and *succubi*, including *incubæ* and *succubæ*, see the *Liber Demonorum* of Protassus (Paris, 1328), which contains much curious information that would be out of place in a dictionary intended as a text-book for the public schools. Victor Hugo relates that in the Channel Islands Satan himself — tempted more than elsewhere by the beauty of the women, doubtless — sometimes plays at *incubus*, greatly to the inconvenience and alarm of the good dames who wish to be loyal to their marriage vows, generally speaking. A certain lady applied to the parish priest to learn how they might, in the dark, distinguish the hardy intruder from their husbands. The holy man said they must feel his brow for horns; but Hugo is ungallant enough to hint a doubt of the efficacy of the test.

INCUMBENT, *n.* A person of the liveliest interest to the outcumbents.

INDECISION, *n.* The chief element of success; "for whereas," saith Sir Thomas Brewbold, "there is but one way to do nothing and divers ways to do something, whereof, to a surety, only one is the right way, it followeth that he who from indecision standeth still hath not so many chances of going astray as he who pusheth forwards"—a most clear and satisfactory exposition of the matter.

"Your prompt decision to attack," said Gen. Grant on a certain occasion to Gen. Gordon Granger, "was admirable; you had but five minutes to make up your mind in."

"Yes, sir," answered the victorious subordinate, "it is a great thing to know exactly what to do in an emergency. When in doubt whether to attack or retreat I never hesitate a moment—I toss up a copper."

"Do you mean to say that 's what you did this time?"

"Yes, General; but for heaven's sake don't reprimand me: I disobeyed the judgment."

INDIFFERENT, *adj.* Imperfectly sensible to distinctions among things.

> "You tiresome man!" cried Indolentio's wife,
> "You 've grown indifferent to all in life."
> "Indifferent?" he drawled with a slow smile;
> "I would be, dear, but it is not worth while."
>
> *Apuleius M. Gokul.*

INDIGESTION, *n.* A disease which the patient and his friends frequently mistake for deep religious conviction and concern for the salvation of mankind. As the simple Red Man of the western wild put it, with, it must be confessed, a certain force: "Plenty well, no pray; big bellyache, heap God."

INDISCRETION, *n.* The guilt of woman.

INEXPEDIENT, *adj.* Not calculated to advance one's interests.

INFANCY, *n.* The period of our lives when, according to Wordsworth, "Heaven lies about us." The world begins lying about us pretty soon afterward.

INFERIÆ, *n.* [Latin.] Among the Greeks and Romans, sacrifices for propitiation of the *Dii Manes*, or souls of dead heroes; for the pious ancients could not invent enough gods to satisfy their spiritual needs, and had to have a number of makeshift deities, or, as a sailor might say, jury-gods, which they made out of the most unpromising materials. It was while sacrificing a bullock to the spirit of Agamemnon that Laiaides, a priest of Aulis, was favored with an audience of that illustrious warrior's shade, who prophetically recounted to him the birth of Christ and the triumph of Christianity, giving him also a rapid but tolerably complete review of events down to the reign of Saint Louis. The narrative ended abruptly at that point owing to the inconsiderate crowing of a cock, which compelled the ghosted King of Men to scamper back to Hades. There is a fine mediæval flavor to this story, and as it has not been traced back further than Père Brateille, a pious but obscure writer at the court of Saint Louis, we shall probably not err on the side of presumption in considering it apocryphal, though Monsignor Capel's judgment of the matter might be different; and to that I bow—wow.

INFIDEL, *n.* In New York, one who does not believe in the Christian religion; in Constantinople, one who does. (See GIAOUR.) A kind of scoundrel imperfectly reverent of, and niggardly contributory to, divines, ecclesiastics, popes, parsons, canons, monks, mollahs, voodoos, presbyters, hierophants, prelates, obeah-men, abbés, nuns, missionaries, exhorters, deacons, friars, hadjis, high-priests, muezzins, brahmins, medicine-men, confessors, eminences, elders, primates, prebendaries, pilgrims, prophets, imaums, beneficiaries, clerks, vicars-choral, archbishops, bishops, abbots, priors, preachers, padres, abbotesses, caloyers, palmers, curates, patriarchs, bonzes, santons, beadsmen, canonesses, residentiaries, diocesans, deans, subdeans, rural deans, abdals, charm-sellers, archdeacons, hierarchs, class-leaders, incumbents, capitulars, sheiks, talapoins, postulants, scribes, gooroos, precentors, beadles, fakeers, sextons, reverences, revivalists, cenobites, perpetual curates, chaplains, mudjoes, readers, novices, vicars, pastors, rabbis, ulemas, lamas, sacristans, vergers, dervises, lecturers, churchwardens, cardinals, prioresses, suffragans, acolytes, rectors, curés, sophis, muftis, and pumpums.

INFLUENCE, *n.* In politics, a visionary *quo* given in exchange for a substanstantial *quid.*

INFRALAPSARIAN, *n.* One who ventures to believe that Adam need not have sinned unless he had a mind to —in opposition to the Supralapsarians, who hold that that luckless person's fall was decreed from the beginning. Infralapsarians are sometimes called Sublapsarians without material effect upon the importance and lucidity of their views about Adam.

Two theologues once, as they wended their way
To chapel, engaged in colloquial fray —
An earnest logomachy, bitter as gall,
Concerning poor Adam and what made him fall.
"'Twas Predestination," cried one — "for the Lord
Decreed he should fall of his own accord."

"Not so—'t was Free will," the other maintained,
"Which led him to choose what the Lord had
ordained."
So fierce and so fiery grew the debate
That nothing but bloodshed their dudgeon could sate;
So off flew their cassocks and caps to the ground
And, moved by the spirit, their hands went round.
Ere either had proved his theology right
By winning, or even beginning, the fight,
A gray old professor of Latin came by,
A staff in his hand and a scowl in his eye,
And learning the cause of their quarrel (for still
As they clumsily sparred they disputed with skill
Of foreordinational freedom of will)
Cried: "Sirrahs! this reasonless warfare compose:
Atwixt ye's no difference worthy of blows.
The sects ye belong to — I'm ready to swear
Ye wrongly interpret the names that they bear.
You — Infralapsarian son of a clown! —
Should only contend that Adam slipped down;
While *you* — you Supralapsarian pup! —
Should nothing aver but that Adam slipped up."

It's all the same whether up or down
You slip on a peel of banana brown;
And Adam analyzed not his blunder
But thought he had slipped on a peal of thunder!
G. J.

INGRATE, *n.* One who receives a benefit from another, or is otherwise an object of charity.

"All men are ingrates," sneered the cynic.
"Nay,"
The good philanthropist replied;
"I did great service to a man one day
Who never since has cursed me to repay,
Nor vilified."

"Ho!" cried the cynic, "lead me to him straight —
With veneration I am overcome,
And fain would have his blessing." "Sad your fate —
He cannot bless you, for I grieve to state
The man is dumb."

Arel Selp.

INJURY, *n.* An offense next in degree of enormity to a slight.

INJUSTICE, *n.* A burden which of all those that we load upon others and carry ourselves is lightest in the hands and heaviest upon the back.

INK, *n.* A villainous compound of tannogallate of iron, gum-arabic, and water, chiefly used to facilitate the infection of idiocy and promote intellectual crime. The properties of ink are peculiar and contradictory: it may be used to make reputations and unmake them; to blacken them and to make them white; but it is most generally and acceptably employed as a mortar to bind together the stones in an edifice of fame, and as a whitewash to conceal afterward the rascal quality of the material. There are men called journalists who have established ink baths which some persons pay money to get into, others to get out of. Not infrequently it occurs that a person who has paid to get in pays twice as much to get out.

INNATE, *adj.* Natural; inherent—as, innate ideas, that is to say, ideas that we are born with, having had them previously imparted to us. The doctrine of innate ideas is one of the most admirable faiths of philosophy, being itself an innate idea and therefore inaccessible to disproof, though

Locke foolishly supposed himself to have given it "a black eye." Among innate ideas may be mentioned the belief in one's ability to conduct a newspaper, in the greatness of one's country, in the superiority of one's civilization, in the importance of one's personal affairs and in the interesting nature of one's diseases.

IN'ARDS, *n.* The stomach, heart, soul, and other bowels. Many eminent investigators do not class the soul as an in'ard, but that acute observer and renowned authority, Dr. Gunsaulus, is persuaded that the mysterious organ known as the spleen is nothing less than our immortal part. To the contrary, Professor Garrett P. Serviss holds that man's soul is that prolongation of his spinal marrow which forms the pith of his no tail; and for demonstration of his faith points confidently to the fact that tailed animals have no souls. Concerning these two theories, it is best to suspend judgment by believing both.

INSCRIPTION, *n.* Something written on another thing. Inscriptions are of many kinds, but mostly memorial, intended to commemorate the fame of some illustrious person and hand down to distant ages the record of his services and virtues. To this class of inscriptions belongs the name of John Smith, pencilled on the Washington monument. Following are examples of memorial inscriptions on tombstones:

> "In the sky my soul is found,
> And my body in the ground.
> By and by my body 'll rise
> To join my spirit in the skies,
> Soaring up to Heaven's gate.
> 1878."

"Sacred to the memory of Jeremiah Tree. Cut down May 9th, 1862, aged 27 yrs. 4 mos. and 12 ds. Indigenous."

"Affliction sore long time she boar,
Phisicians was in vain,
Till Deth released the dear deceased
And left her a remain.
Gone to join Ananias and Saphiar in the regions of bliss."

"The clay which rests beneath this stone
As Silas Wood was widely known.
Now, lying here, I ask what good
It was to me to be S. Wood.
O Man, let not ambition trouble you
Is the advice of Silas W."

"Richard Haymon, of Heaven, fell to Earth Jan. 20, 1807, and had the dust brushed off him Oct. 3, 1874."

INSECTIVORA, *n.*

"See," cries the chorus of admiring preachers,
"How Providence provides for all His creatures!"
"His care," the gnat said, "even the insects follows:
For us He has provided wrens and swallows."

Sempen Railey.

INSURANCE, *n.* An ingenious modern game of chance in which the player is permitted to enjoy the comfortable conviction that he is beating the man who keeps the table.

INSURANCE AGENT: My dear sir, that is a fine house — pray let me insure it.

HOUSE OWNER: With pleasure. Please make the annual premium so low that by the time when, according to the tables of your actuary, it will probably be destroyed by fire I will have paid you considerably less than the face of the policy.

INSURANCE AGENT: O dear, no — we could not afford to do that. We must fix the premium so that you will have paid more.

HOUSE OWNER: How, then, can *I* afford *that?*

INSURANCE AGENT: Why, your house may burn down at any time. There was Smith's house, for example, which —

HOUSE OWNER: Spare me — there were Brown's house, on the contrary, and Jones's house, and Robinson's house, which —

INSURANCE AGENT: Spare *me!*

HOUSE OWNER: Let us understand each other. You want me to pay you money on the supposition that something will occur previously to the time set by yourself for its occurrence. In other words, you expect me to bet that my house will not last so long as it will probably last.

Insurance Agent: But if your house burns without insurance it will be a total loss.

House Owner: Beg your pardon — by your own actuary's tables I shall probably have saved, when it burns, all the premiums I would otherwise have paid to you — amounting to more than the face of the policy they would have bought. But suppose it to burn before the time upon which your figures are based. If I could afford that, how could you?

Insurance Agent: Oh, we would make ourselves even from our luckier ventures with other clients. Virtually, they pay your loss.

House Owner: And virtually, then, don't I help to pay their losses? Are not their houses as likely as mine to burn before they have paid you as much as you must pay them? The case stands this way: You expect to take more money from your clients than you pay to them, do you not?

Insurance Agent: Certainly; if we did not —

House Owner: I would not trust

you with my money unless you did. Very well, then. If it is *certain*, with reference to the whole body of your clients, that they lose money on you it is *probable*, with reference to any one of them, that *he* will. It is these individual probabilities that make the aggregate certainty.

INSURANCE AGENT: I will not deny it—but look at the figures in this pamph—

HOUSE OWNER: Heaven forbid!

INSURANCE AGENT: You spoke of saving the premiums which you would otherwise pay to me. Will you not be more likely to squander them? We offer you an incentive to thrift.

HOUSE OWNER: The willingness of A to take care of B's money is not peculiar to insurance, but as a charitable institution you command esteem. Deign to accept its expression from a Deserving Object.

INSURRECTION, *n.* An unsuccessful revolution; disaffection's failure to substitute misrule for bad government.

INTENTION, *n.* The mind's sense of the prevalence of one set of influences over another set; an effect whose cause is the imminence, immediate or remote, of the performance of an involuntary act.

INTERPRETER, *n.* One who enables two persons of different languages to understand each other by repeating to each what it would have been to the interpreter's advantage for the other to have said.

INTERREGNUM, *n.* The period during which a monarchical country is governed by a warm spot on the cushion of the throne. The experiment of letting the spot grow cold has commonly been attended by most unhappy results from the zeal of many worthy persons to keep it warm.

INTIMACY, *n.* A relation into which fools are providentially drawn for their mutual destruction.

Two Seidlitz powders, one in blue
And one in white, together drew,
And having each a pleasant sense
Of t' other powder's excellence,
Forsook their jackets for the snug
Enjoyment of a common mug.
So close their intimacy grew
One paper would have held the two.
To confidences straight they fell,
Less anxious each to hear than tell;
Then each remorsefully confessed
To all the virtues he possessed,
Acknowledging he had them in
So high degree it was a sin.
The more they said, the more they felt
Their spirits with emotion melt,
Till tears in cataracts expressed
Their feelings. Then they effervesced!

So Nature executes her feats
Of wrath on friends and sympathetes
The good old rule who won't apply,
That you are you and I am I.

INTRODUCTION, *n.* A social ceremony invented by the devil for the gratification of his servants and the plaguing of his enemies. The introduction attains in this country its most malevolent development, being, indeed, closely related to our political system. Every American being the equal of every other American, it follows that everybody has the right to know everybody else, which implies the right to introduce without request or permission. The Declaration of Independence should have read thus:

"We hold these truths to be self-evident: that all men are created nice and equal; that they are endowed by their Creator with certain inalienable rights; that among these are life, and the right to make that of another miserable by thrusting upon him an incalculable quantity of acquaintances; liberty, particularly the liberty to introduce persons to one another without first ascertaining if they are not already acquainted as enemies; and the pursuit of another's happiness with a running pack of strangers."

INVENTOR, *n.* A person who makes an ingenious arrangement of wheels, levers, and springs, and believes it civilization.

IRRELIGION, *n.* The principal one of the great faiths of the world.

ITCH, *n.* The patriotism of a Scotchman.

J

J is a consonant in English, but some nations use it as a vowel — than which nothing could be more absurd. Its original form, which has been but slightly modified, was that of the tail of a subdued dog, and it was not a letter but a character, standing for the Latin verb *jacere*, "to throw," because when a stone is thrown at a dog the dog's tail assumes that shape. This is the origin of the letter, as expounded by the learned and renowned Dr. Jocolpus Bumer, of the University of Belgrade, who established his conclusions on the subject in a work of three quarto volumes and committed suicide on being reminded that the j in the Roman alphabet had originally no curl.

JEALOUS, *adj.* Unduly concerned about the preservation of that which can only be lost if not worth keeping.

JESTER, *n.* An officer formerly attached to a king's household, whose business it was to amuse the court by ludicrous actions and utterances, the absurdity being attested by his motley costume. The king himself being attired with dignity, it took the world some centuries to discover that his own conduct and decrees were sufficiently ridiculous for the amusement not only of his court but of all mankind. The jester was commonly called a fool, but the poets and romancers have ever delighted to represent him as a singularly wise and witty person. In the circus clown of to-day the melancholy ghost of the court fool effects the dejection of humbler audiences with the same jests wherewith in life he gloomed the marble hall, panged the patrician sense of humor and tapped the tank of royal tears.

The widow-queen of Portugal
  Had an audacious jester
Who entered the confessional
  Disguised and there confessed her.

"Father," she said, "thine ear bend down —
  My sins are more than scarlet:
I love my fool — blaspheming clown,
  And common, base-born varlet."

"Daughter," the mimic priest replied,
  "That sin, indeed, is awful:
The church's pardon is denied
  To love that is unlawful.

"But since thy stubborn heart will be
  For him forever pleading,
Thou 'dst better make him, by decree,
  A man of birth and breeding."

She made the fool a duke, in hope
  With Heaven's taboo to palter;
Then told the priest, who told the pope,
  Who damned her from the altar!

Barel Dort.

JEWS-HARP, *n.* An unmusical instrument, played by holding it fast with the teeth and trying to brush it away with the finger.

JOSS-STICKS, *n.* Small sticks burned by the Chinese in their pagan tomfoolery, in imitation of certain sacred rites of our holy religion.

JUSTICE, *n.* A commodity which in a more or less adulterated condition the State sells to the citizen as a reward for his allegiance, taxes, and personal service.

K

K is a consonant that we get from the Greeks, but it can be traced away back beyond them to the Cerathians, a small commercial nation inhabiting the peninsula of Smero. In their tongue it was called *Klatch*, which means "destroyed." The form of the letter was originally precisely that of our H, but the erudite and ingenious Dr. Snedeker explains that it was altered to its present shape to commemorate the destruction of the great temple of Jarute by an earthquake, *circa* 730 B. C. This building was famous for the two lofty columns of its portico, one of which was broken in half by the catastrophe, the other remaining intact. As the earlier form of the letter is supposed to have been suggested by these pillars, so, it is thought by the great antiquary, its later was adopted as a simple and natural — not to say touching — means of keeping the calamity ever in the national memory. It is not known if the name of the letter was altered as an additional mnemonic, or if the name was always *Klatch* and the destruction one of nature's puns. As each theory seems probable enough, I see no objection to believing both — and Dr. Snedeker arrayed himself on that side of the question.

KEEP, *v. t.*

He willed away his whole estate,
And then in death he fell asleep,
Murmuring: "Well, at any rate,
My name unblemished I shall keep."

But when upon the tomb 't was wrought
Whose was it? — for the dead keep naught.

Durang Gophel Arn.

KILL, *v. t.* To create a vacancy without nominating a successor.

KILT, *n.* A costume affected by Scotchmen in America and Americans in Scotland.

KINDNESS, *n.* A brief preface to ten volumes of exaction.

KING, *n.* A male person commonly known in America as a "crowned head," although he never wears a crown and has usually no head to speak of.

A king, in times long, long gone by,
  Said to his lazy jester:
"If I were you and you were I
My moments merrily would fly —
  No care nor grief to pester."

"The reason, Sire, that you would thrive,"
  The fool said — "if you 'll hear it —
Is that of all the fools alive
Who own you for their sovereign, I 've
  The most forgiving spirit."

Oogum Bem.

KING'S EVIL, *n.* A malady that was formerly cured by the touch of the sovereign, but has now to be treated by the physicians. Thus "the most pious Edward" of England used to lay his royal hand upon his ailing subjects and make them whole —

"a crowd of wretched souls
That stay his cure: their malady convinces
The great essay of art; but at his touch,
Such sanctity hath Heaven given his hand
They presently amend,"

as the "Doctor" in *Macbeth* hath it. This useful property of the royal hand could, it appears, be transmitted along with other crown properties; for according to "Malcolm,"

> "'t is spoken,
> To the succeeding royalty he leaves
> The healing benediction."

But the gift somewhere dropped out of the line of succession: the later sovereigns of England have not been tactual healers, and the disease once honored with the name "king's evil" now bears the humbler one of "scrofula," from *scrofa*, a sow. The date and author of the following epigram are unknown, but it is old enough to show that the jest about Scotland's national disorder is not a thing of yesterday.

> Ye Kynge his evill in me laye,
> Wh. he of Scottlande charmed awaye.
> He layde his hand on mine and sayd:
> "Be gone!" Ye ill no longer stayd.
> But O ye wofull plyght in wh.
> I'm now y-pight: I have ye itche!

The superstition that maladies can be cured by royal taction is dead, but like many a departed conviction it has left a monument of custom to keep its memory green. The practice of forming in line and shaking the President's hand had no other origin, and when that great dignitary bestows his healing salutation on

> "strangely visited people,
> All swoln and ulcerous, pitiful to the eye,
> The mere despair of surgery,"

he and his patients are handing along an extinguished torch which once was kindled at the altar-fire of a faith long held by all classes of men. It is a beautiful and edifying "survival" — one which brings the sainted past very close home to our "business and bosoms."

KISS, *n.* A word invented by the poets as a rhyme for "bliss." It is supposed to signify, in a general way, some kind of rite or ceremony appertaining to a good understanding; but the manner of its performance is unknown to the author of this dictionary.

KLEPTOMANIAC, *n.* A rich thief.

KNIGHT, *n.*

Once a warrior gentle of birth,
Then a person of civic worth,
Now a fellow to move our mirth.
Warrior, person, and fellow — no more:
We must knight our dogs to get any lower.
Brave Knights Kennelers then shall be,
Noble Knights of the Golden Flea,
Knights of the Order of St. Steboy,
Knights of St. Gorge and Knights of Jawy.
God speed the day when this knighting fad
Shall go to the dogs and the dogs go mad.

KORAN, *n.* A book which the Mohammedans foolishly believe to have been written by divine inspiration, but which Christians know to be a wicked imposture, contradictory to the Holy Scriptures.

L

LABOR, *n.* One of the processes by which A acquires property for B.

LACE, *n.* A delicate and costly textile fabric with which the female soul is netted like a fish.

> The devil casting a seine of lace
> (With precious stones 't was weighted)
> Drew it in to the landing place
> And its contents calculated.
>
> All souls of women were in that sack —
> A draught miraculous, precious!
> But ere he could throw it across his back
> They 'd all escaped through the meshes.
>
> *Baruch de Loppis.*

LAND, *n.* A part of the earth's surface, considered as property. The theory that land is property subject to private ownership and control is the foundation of modern society, and is eminently worthy of the superstructure. Carried to its logical conclusion, it means that some have the right to prevent others from living; for the right to own implies the right exclusively to occupy, and in fact laws of trespass are enacted wherever property in land is recognized. It follows that if the whole area of *terra firma* is owned by A, B, and C, there will be no place for D, E, F, and G to be born on, or, being born as trespassers, to exist on.

> A life on the ocean wave,
>   A home on the rolling deep,
> For the spark that nature gave
>   I have there the right to keep.
>
> They give me the cat-o'-nine
>   Whenever I go ashore.
> Then ho! for the flashing brine—
>   I'm a natural commodore!
>
> *Dodle.*

LANGUAGE, *n.* The music with which we charm the serpents guarding another's treasure.

LAOCOÖN, *n.* A famous piece of antique sculpture representing a priest of that name and his two sons in the folds of two enormous serpents. The skill and diligence with which the old man and lads support the serpents and keep them up to their work have been justly regarded as one of the noblest artistic illustrations of the mastery of human intelligence over brute inertia.

LAP, *n.* One of the most important organs of the female system — an admirable provision of nature for the repose of infancy, but chiefly useful in rural festivities to support plates of cold chicken and heads of adult males. The male of our species has a rudimentary lap, imperfectly developed and in no way contributing to the animal's substantial welfare.

LAST, *n.* A shoemaker's implement, named by a frowning Providence as opportunity to the maker of puns.

> Ah, punster, would my lot were cast,
> Where the cobbler is unknown,
> So that I might forget his last
> And hear your own.
>
> *Gargo Repsky.*

LAUGHTER, *n.* An interior convulsion, producing a distortion of the features and accompanied by inarticulate noises. It is infectious and, though intermittent, incurable. Liability to attacks of laughter is one of the characteristics distinguishing man from the animals — these being not only inaccessible to the provocation of his example, but impregnable to the microbes having original jurisdiction in bestowal of the disease. Whether laughter could be imparted to animals by inoculation from the human patient is a question that has not been answered by experimentation. Dr. Weir Mitchell holds that the infectious character of laughter is due to instantaneous fermentation of *sputa* diffused in a spray. From this peculiarity he names the disorder *Convulsio spargens*.

LAUREATE, *adj.* Crowned with the leaves of the vegetable aforesaid. In

England the Poet Laureate is an officer of the sovereign's court, acting as dancing skeleton at every royal feast and singing mute at every royal funeral. Of all incumbents of that high office Robert Southey had the most notable knack at drugging the Samson of public joy and cutting his hair to the quick; and he had an artistic color-sense which enabled him so to blacken a public grief as to give it the aspect of a national crime.

LAUREL, *n.* The *laurus*, a vegetable dedicated to Apollo, and formerly defoliated to wreathe the brows of victors and such poets as had influence at court.

LAW, *n.*

Once Law was sitting on the bench,
And Mercy knelt a-weeping.
"Clear out!" he cried, "disordered wench!
Nor come before me creeping.
Upon your knees if you appear,
'T is plain you have no standing here."

Then Justice came. His Honor cried:
"*Your* status? — devil seize you!"
"*Amica curiæ*," she replied —
"Friend of the court, so please you."
"Begone!" he shouted — "there's the door —
I never saw your face before!"

G. J.

LAWFUL, *adj.* Compatible with the will of a judge having jurisdiction.

LAWYER, *n.* One skilled in circumvention of the law. One of the chief duties of the modern lawyer is defense of eminent rogues by vituperation of "anonymous scribblers" of the press — an employment which drew from that "scurril jester," Editor Fum, of "The Daily Livercomplaint," the hortatory words here following:

Take notice, lawyers all. For many a year
Your cheerful tribe (I mean to stint your cheer)
When hired to cheat the gallows of its prey
Or turn the law-dogs' noses all astray
From a thief's track, and take of what he stole
The lion's share — that is to say, the whole —
Have deemed it right his grievance to redress

With fine philippics on the brutal press
That persecutes a blameless soul — alas,
How angels suffer from the felon class!
Now mark ye, lawless lawyers, if ye still
Shall think it well to serve a client ill,
Accept his money on the false pretense
That slander of accusers is defense,
Deal out damnation to sustain his hope
And handle without gloves all things but soap,
I'm for retaliation. Hear me swear,
With head uncovered and with hand in air,
By that sole deity whom lawyers hold
In pious reverence, Almighty Gold
(Whose name, with deep hypocrisy, they spell,
Pronounce and take in vain without the l)
My scourging weapon shall remain unstirred,
Gracing the pinion of its parent bird.
I'll let you struggle for the blackguard's wreath
And tear your tongues to rags upon your teeth!

LAZINESS, *n.* Unwarranted repose of manner in a person of low degree.

LEAD, *n.* A heavy blue-gray metal much used in giving stability to light lovers — particularly to those who love not wisely but other men's wives. Lead is also of great service as a counterpoise to an argument of such weight that it turns the scale of debate the wrong way. An interesting fact in the chemistry of international controversy is that at the point of contact of two patriotisms lead is precipitated in great quantities.

Hail, holy Lead! — of human feuds the great
  And universal arbiter; endowed
  With penetration to pierce any cloud
Fogging the field of controversial hate,
And with a swift, inevitable, straight,
  Searching precision find the unavowed
  But vital point. Thy judgment, when allowed
By the chirurgeon, settles the debate.
O useful metal! — were it not for thee
  We'd grapple one another's ears alway:
But when we hear thee buzzing like a bee
  We, like old Muhlenberg, "care not to stay."
And when the quick have run away like pullets
Jack Satan smelts the dead to make new bullets.

LEARNING, *n.* The kind of ignorance distinguishing the studious.

LECTURER, *n.* One with his hand in your pocket, his tongue in your ear, and his faith in your patience.

LEGACY, *n.* A gift from one who is legging it out of this vale of tears.

LEONINE, *adj.* Unlike a menagerie lion. Leonine verses are those in which a word in the middle rhymes with a word at the end, as in this famous passage from Bella Peeler Silcox:

The electric light invades the dunnest deep of Hades.
Cries Pluto, 'twixt his snores: "O tempora! O mores!"

It should be explained that Mrs. Silcox does not undertake to teach the pronunciation of the Greek and Latin tongues. Leonine verses are so called in honor of a poet named Leo, whom prosodists appear to find a pleasure in believing to have been the first to discover that a rhyming couplet could be run into a single line.

LETTUCE, *n.* An herb of the genus *Lactuca*, "wherewith," says that pious gastronome, Hengist Pelly, "God has been pleased to reward the good and punish the wicked. For by his inner light the righteous man has discerned a manner of compounding for it a dressing to the appetency whereof a multitude of gustible condiments conspire, being reconciled and ameliorated with profusion of oil, the entire comestible making glad the heart of the godly and causing his face to shine. But the person of spiritual unworth is successfully tempted of the Adversary to eat of the lettuce with destitution of oil, mustard, egg, salt, and garlic, and with a rascal bath of vinegar polluted with sugar. Wherefore the person of spiritual unworth suffers an intestinal pang of strange complexity and raises the song."

LEVIATHAN, *n.* An enormous aquatic animal mentioned by Job. Some suppose it to have been the whale, but that distinguished ichthyologer, Dr. Jordan, of Stanford University, maintains with considerable heat that it was a species of gigantic Tadpole, (*Thaddeus Polandensis*) or Polliwig — *Maria pseudo-hirsuta*. For an exhaustive description and history of the Tadpole consult the famous monograph of Jane Porter, *Thaddeus of Warsaw*.

LEXICOGRAPHER, *n.* A pestilent fellow who, under the pretense of recording some particular stage in the development of a language, does what he can to arrest its growth, stiffen its flexibility, and mechanize its methods. For your lexicographer, having written his dictionary, comes to be considered "as one having authority," whereas his function is only to make a record, not to give a law. The natural servility of the human understanding having invested him with judicial power, surrenders its right of reason and submits itself to a chronicle as if it were a statute. Let the dictionary (for example) mark a good word as "obsolete" or "obsolescent" and no man thereafter ventures to use it, whatever his need of it and however desirable its restoration to favor — whereby the process of impoverishment is accelerated and speech decays. On the contrary, the bold and discerning writer who, recognizing the truth that language must grow by innovation if it grow at all, makes new words and uses the old in an unfamiliar sense has no following and is tartly reminded that "it is n't in the dictionary" — although down to the time of the first lexicographer (Heaven forgive him!) no author ever had used a word that *was* in the dictionary. In the golden prime and high noon of English speech; when from the lips of the great Elizabethans fell words that made their own meaning and carried it in their very sound; when a Shakespeare and a Bacon were possible, and the language now rapidly perishing at one end and slowly renewed at the other was in vigorous growth and hardy preservation — sweeter than honey and stronger than a lion — the lexicographer was a person unknown, the dictionary a creation which his Creator had not created him to create.

God said: "Let Spirit perish into Form,"
And lexicographers arose, a swarm!
Thought fled and left her clothing, which they took
And catalogued each garment in a book.
Now, from her leafy covert when she cries:
"Give me my clothes and I 'll return," they rise
And scan the list, and say without compassion:
"Excuse us — they are mostly out of fashion."

Sigismund Smith.

LIAR, *n.* A lawyer with a roving commission.

LIBERTY, *n.* One of Imagination's most precious possessions.

The rising People, hot and out of breath,
Roared round the palace: "Liberty or death!"
"If death will do," the King said, "let me reign;
You'll have, I'm sure, no reason to complain."

Martha Braymance.

LICKSPITTLE, *n.* A useful functionary, not infrequently found editing a newspaper. In his character of editor he is closely allied to the blackmailer by the tie of occasional identity; for in truth the lickspittle is only the blackmailer under another aspect, though the latter is frequently found as an independent species. Lickspittling is more detestable than blackmailing, precisely as the business of a confidence man is more detestable than that of a highway robber; and the parallel maintains itself throughout, for whereas few robbers will cheat, every sneak will plunder if he dare.

LIFE, *n.* A spiritual pickle preserving the body from decay. We live in daily apprehension of its loss; yet when lost it is not missed. The question, "Is life worth living?" has been much discussed; particularly by those who think it is not, many of whom have written at great length in support of their view and by careful observance of the laws of health enjoyed for long terms of years the honors of successful controversy.

> "Life 's not worth living, and that 's the truth,"
> Carelessly caroled the golden youth;
> And in manhood still he maintained that view
> And held it more strongly the older he grew.
> When kicked by a jackass at eighty-three,
> "Go fetch me a surgeon at once!" cried he.
>
> *Han Soper.*

LIGHTHOUSE, *n.* A tall building on the seashore in which the government maintains a lamp and the friend of a politician.

LIMB, *n.* The branch of a tree or the leg of an American woman.

'T was a pair of boots that the lady bought,
And the salesman laced them tight
To a very remarkable height —
Higher, indeed, than I think he ought —
Higher than *can* be right.
For the Bible declares — but never mind:
It is hardly fit
To censure freely and fault to find
With others for sins that I 'm not inclined
Myself to commit.
Each has his weakness, and though my own
Is freedom from every sin,
It still were unfair to pitch in,
Discharging the first censorious stone.
Besides, the truth compels me to say,
The boots in question were *made* that way.
As he drew the lace she made a grimace,
And blushingly said to him:
" This boot, I 'm sure, is too high to endure,
It hurts my — hurts my — limb."
The salesman smiled in a manner mild,
Like an artless, undesigning child;
Then, checking himself, to his face he gave
A look as sorrowful as the grave,
Though he did n't care two figs
For her pains and throes,
As he stroked her toes,
Remarking with speech and manner just
Befitting his calling: " Madam, I trust
That it does n't hurt your twigs."

G. Percival Doke.

LINEN, *n.* "A kind of cloth the making of which entails a great waste of hemp." — *Calcraft the Hangman.*

LITIGANT, *n.* A person about to give up his skin for the hope of retaining his bones.

LITIGATION, *n.* A machine which you go into as a pig and come out of as a sausage.

LIVER, *n.* A large red organ thoughtfully provided by nature to be bilious with. The sentiments and emotions which every literary anatomist now knows to haunt the heart were anciently believed to infest the liver; and even Gascoygne, speaking of the emotional side of human nature, calls it "our hepaticall parte." It was at one time considered the seat of life; hence its name — liver, the thing we live with. The liver is heaven's best gift to the goose; without it that bird would be unable to supply us with the Strasbourg *pâté*.

LL.D. Letters indicating the degree *Legumptionis Doctor*, one learned in the laws, gifted with legal gumption. Some suspicion is cast upon this derivation by the fact that the title was formerly *££. d.*, and conferred only upon gentlemen distinguished for their wealth. At the date of this writing Columbia University is considering the expediency of making another degree for clergymen, in place of the old D.D. — *Damnator Diaboli*. The new honor will be known as *Sanctorum Custos*, and written $$. ¢. The name of the Rev. John Satan has been suggested as a suitable recipient by a lover of consistency, who points out that Professor Harry Thurston Peck has long enjoyed the advantage of a degree.

LOCK-AND-KEY, *n.* The distinguishing device of civilization and enlightenment.

LODGER, *n.* A less popular name for the First Person of that delectable newspaper Trinity, the Roomer, the Bedder, and the Mealer.

LOGIC, *n.* The art of thinking and reasoning in strict accordance with the limitations and incapacities of the human misunderstanding. The basis of logic is the syllogism, consisting of a major and a minor premise and a conclusion — thus:

Major Premise: Sixty men can do a piece of work sixty times as quickly as one man.

Minor Premise: One man can dig a post-hole in sixty seconds; therefore—

Conclusion: Sixty men can dig a post-hole in one second.

This may be called the syllogism arithmetical, in which, by combining logic and mathematics, we obtain a double certainty and are twice blessed.

LORD, *n.* In American society, an English tourist above the state of a costermonger, as, Lord 'Aberdasher, Lord Hartisan, and so forth. The travelling Briton of lesser degree is addressed as "Sir," as, Sir 'Arry Donkiboi, of 'Amstead 'Eath. The word "Lord" is sometimes used, also, as a title of the Supreme Being; but this is thought to be rather flattery than true reverence.

Miss Sallie Ann Splurge, of her own accord,
Wedded a wandering English lord —
Wedded and took him to dwell with her "paw,"
A parent who throve by the practice of Draw.
Lord Cadde I don't hesitate here to declare
Unworthy the father-in-legal care
Of that elderly sport, notwithstanding the truth
That Cadde had renounced the follies of youth;
For, sad to relate, he 'd arrived at the stage
Of existence that 's marked by the vices of age.
Among them cupidity caused him to urge
Repeated demands on the pocket of Splurge,
Till, wrecked in his fortune, that gentleman saw
Inadequate aid in the practice of Draw,
And took, as a means of augmenting his pelf,
To the business of being a lord himself.
His neat-fitting garments he willfully shed
And sacked himself strangely in checks instead;
Denuded his chin, but retained at each ear
A whisker that looked like a blasted career.

He painted his neck an incarnadine hue
Each morning and varnished it all that he knew.
The moony monocular set in his eye
Appeared to be scanning the Sweet Bye-and-Bye.
His head was enroofed with a billycock hat,
And his low-necked shoes were aduncous and flat.
In speech he eschewed his American ways,
Denying his nose to the use of his A's
And dulling their edge till the delicate sense
Of a babe at their temper could take no offence.
His H's — 't was most inexpressibly sweet,
The patter they made as they fell at his feet!
Re-outfitted thus, Mr. Splurge without fear
Began as Lord Splurge his recouping career.
Alas, the Divinity shaping his end
Entertained other views and decided to send
His lordship in horror, despair, and dismay
From the land of the nobleman's natural prey.
For, smit with his Old World ways, Lady Cadde
Fell — suffering Caesar! — in love with her dad!

G. J.

www.ingramcontent.com/pod-product-compliance
Ingram Content Group UK Ltd.
Pitfield, Milton Keynes, MK11 3LW, UK
UKHW020223250726
13967UKWH00001B/151

9 781435 749320